Sukhoi Su-30
Super Manoeuvrable Family
MKI/MKM/MKI(A)/SM

Hugh Harkins

Copyright © 2016 Hugh Harkins

All rights reserved.

ISBN: 1-903630-59-2
ISBN-13: 978-1-903630-59-4

Sukhoi Su-30
Super Manoeuvrable Family
MKI/MKM/MKI(A)/SM

© Hugh Harkins 2016

Published by Centurion Publishing
United Kingdom

ISBN 10: 1-903630-59-2
ISBN 13: 978-1-903630-59-4

This volume first published in 2016
The Author is identified as the copyright holder of this work under sections
77 and 78 of the Copyright Designs and Patents Act 1988

Cover design © Centurion Publishing & Createspace

Page layout, concept and design © Centurion Publishing

All rights reserved. No part of this publication may be reproduced, stored in
a retrieval system, transmitted in any form, or by any means, electronic,
mechanical or photocopied, recorded or otherwise, without the written
permission of the Publisher

The Publisher and Author would like to thank all organisations and services for their assistance and contributions in the preparation of this volume. JSC Sukhoi Design Bureau (Sukhoi Aviation Holding Company), United Aircraft Corporation, NPO Saturn, United Engine Corporation, JSC V. Tikhomirov NIIP, Zhukovsky, JSC Tactical Missiles Corporation, JSC Concern Radio-Electronic Technologies (KRET), JSC Ramenskoye Design Bureau (RPBK), Rostec Corporation, KnAAPO, BrahMos Aerospace, NPP Zvezda, Hindustan Aeronautics Limited (HAL), Saab Group, the Ministry of Defence of the Russian Federation and the Indian Air Force

CONTENTS

	INTRODUCTION	i
1	Su-30MK DESIGN GENESIS	1
2	Su-30MK DEMONSTRATOR & Su-30K INTERIM EXPORT FIGHTER	17
3	Su-30MK SUPER-MANOEUVRABLE FAMILY – Su-30MKI/Su-30MKM/Su-30MKI(A)	27
4	Su-30MKI/MKM/MKI(A) PRODUCTION AND SERVICE	65
5	Su-30SM(CM) – RUSSIAN DOMESTIC SUPER-MANOEUVRABLE FIGHTER	85
6	ADVANCED WEAPONS PLATFORM	105
7	RUSSIAN AEROSPACE GROUP Su-30SM OPERATIONS OVER SYRIA	125
8	SUPER-MANOEUVRABILITY – $4^{th}+/4^{th}++/5^{th}$ GENERATION NECESSITY OR LUXURY?	143
9	APPENDICES	151
10	GLOSSARY	154

INTRODUCTION

The Su-30MKI family of super-manoeuvrable multi-role combat aircraft share the same numerical designation as the Su-30MKK/MK2 family of combat aircraft although both design groups, despite being directly descendant from the first generation Su-27, took different evolutionary paths. Numerical designation and some first glance looks aside, the Su-30MKI family are fundamentally different designs from the Su-30MKK/MK2 family in terms of primary design role, internal systems and structure; certainly in regards to the latter the Su-30MKK/MK2 having more in common with the Su-27M (first generation Su-35) than the Su-30M from which the Su-30MKI is clearly derived; this design clearly having evolved from the Su-30M which was developed from the Su-27UB two-seat operational conversion trainer variant of the Su-27S single-seat air superiority fighter.

This volume covers the evolution of the Su-30 design from the Su-27, which was born out of the T-10 development program of the 1970's. The evolution of the Su-30M interceptor into the multi-role Su-30MK and ergo the Su-30MKI 'super-manoeuvrable' series is detailed.

The various design models, the Su-30MKI for India, Su-30MKM for Malaysia, Su-30MKI(A) for Algeria and the domesticated Su-30SM (Russian CM) for Russia and Kazakhstan are described in detail, as are the weapons that can be employed by the respective variants.

All technical information regarding the aircraft, systems and weapons have been provided by the respective manufacturers, as have many of the photographs and graphics. Certain elements of text, when pertinent, are taken from the volumes 'Sukhoi Su-35S 'Flanker' E, Russia's 4++ Generation Super-Manoeuvrability Fighter' and 'Sukhoi T-50/PAK FA, Russia's 5th Generation 'Stealth' Fighter'.

1

SU-30MK DESIGN GENESIS

The design origins of the Sukhoi Su-30MKI 'super manoeuvrable' multi-role fighter family, which encompasses the Su-30MKM, Su-30MKI(A) and Su-30SM, go back to the Sukhoi Su-27 program, the origins of which go back to the Sukhoi T-10, design work on which commenced under the leadership of O.S. Samoilovich in late 1969, when the Sukhoi OBK Design Bureau in the Soviet Union embarked upon studies for a new long range air superiority fighter for the Soviet IA-PVO (*Istrebitelnaya Aviatsiya Protivo-Vozdushnoy Obstrany*/Air Defence Force). While the new fighter would have a stipulated secondary ground attack capability, the aircraft design would be optimised for the primary air superiority mission. Performance requirements for the new fighter included long-range and high manoeuvrability, combined with modern radar and weapon systems to enable the aircraft to be capable of defeating the most modern western fighter aircraft then projected, typified by the McDonnell Douglas (later Boeing) F-15 Eagle then being developed under the FX program.

A number of concepts were studied, various designs being drawn up by the design houses of P.O. Sukhoi, A.I. Mikoyan and A.S. Yakovlev during 1971-1972. The two former design houses were designing high agility aircraft, both arriving at similar configurations, attributed to the fact that both utilised data from the same research agency. The design that eventually became the Mikoyan PFI (Advanced Frontline Fighter) Project 9, therefore, resembled a scaled down version of the Sukhoi T-10, the latter being designed around a highly blended fore-body and high lift ogive wing with LERX (Leading Edge Root Extensions).

The initial design for the T-10 was complete by September 1971, submitted in February 1972, and, following a preliminary review, design revisions were incorporated, following which full-scale development commenced in conjunction with development of a lightweight fighter by Mikoyan; the MiG-29 (Project 9). The Sukhoi and Mikoyan designs were, however, not in competition with each other; the former being planned as a heavy fighter and the latter being planned as a light fighter capable of engaging its NATO opposite numbers.

The Su-30MKI family of 'super-manoeuvrable' combat aircraft can be distinguished from other Su-30 variants by their canard-triplane configuration and thrust vector control for the engine nozzles. UAC

During the course of 1972-73, the T-10 was further redesigned, the changes including increased wing area and fuel capacity. The thrust of the proposed powerplant, A.M. Lyulka (NPO Saturn) AL-31F (Article 99), was increased to compensate for increased weights. By 1975, Sukhoi data described the T-10 design with the following features, "an integrated ogive wing configuration, leading-edge root extensions, an all-moving horizontal tail unit mounted on the centre wing section continuation beams, and twin tail fins mounted on engine nacelles at the airframe stern post". The variable engine intakes were positioned "either side of the plane's roll axis, and suspended from the centre wing section" ensuring a stable air flow to the engines even when the aircraft was flying at high AoA (Angle of Attack).

The T-10 was designed with inherent lateral instability, balanced by an EDCS (Electronic Distance Control System), computerised FBW (Fly-By-Wire) FCS (Flight Control System). The Soviet Union had pioneered FBW technology with the Sukhoi T-4 intermediate range bomber (cancelled in the 1970's), which conducted its first flight on 22 August 1972. The first American combat aircraft designed with a FBW FCS, the General Dynamics YF-16, conducted its maiden flight on 2 February 1974, followed by the first flight of the European Panavia Tornado prototype (then known as the MRCA - Multi-role Combat Aircraft) on 8 August that year. While the T-4 flew before the YF-16 and Tornado, the FBW FCS installed in the Western aircraft were more advanced than the early Soviet system, providing FBW control in all axes.

Top: A rather crude artist depiction of the new Soviet fighters under development in the late 1970's. US DoD **Above: Side on view of the prototype T-10 circa 1977.** NPO

Approval of the T-10 configuration was granted on 19 January 1976. Three prototypes (two flight and one ground test) were under construction by early 1976, the first, T-10-1, being completed in April 1977. This aircraft, along with the second, third and fourth development aircraft, T-10-2, T-10-3 and T-10-4, was built at Sukhoi's experimental plant near Moscow.

Western intelligence agencies got their first glimpse of the new Soviet fighter design from photographs taken by a spy satellite while the aircraft was on the ground at Zhukovsky (then known in the west as Ramenskoye). NATO (North Atlantic Treaty Organisation) allocated the new aircraft the reporting name RAM-K as it was the tenth experimental fighter aircraft observed at the base (the letter I was apparently not used in the RAM reporting sequence). The MiG-29 (Project 9) was allocated the reporting name RAM-L.

Its combination of high aerodynamic/kinetic performance, high agility, long endurance and combat persistence ensured the Su-27's capabilities would be a real concern for NATO planners. This photograph, taken in the mid-1980's, shows a Su-27 carrying six medium range air to air missiles; four R-27R1 semi-active radar guided and two R-27T1 infrared guided. US DoD.

The prototype T-10, which was powered by a pair of AL-21FZAI afterburning turbojet engines, flew for the first time on 20 May 1977, piloted by Sukhoi Chief Test Pilot V.S. Ilyushin. The AL-21FZAI, which was an interim engine rated at 76.49 kN (16,195 lb.) dry and 109.84 kN (21,692 lb.) in afterburner (the available thrust may have been a little higher than these interim ratings), was a derivative of the AL-21F-3 engine that was used to power a number of Soviet combat aircraft, including the Su-17 'Fitter' and the Su-24 'Fencer' variable-geometry strike aircraft. While the dry thrust of the AL-21F-3 was higher than the dry thrust of the AL-31F (Article 99) planned for the productionised T-10 (Su-27), the afterburner thrust was lower and the engine had a much higher specific fuel consumption compared with the AL-31F; a serious consideration for an aircraft designed as a long-range air superiority fighter.

Following construction of the initial batch of four aircraft a further five, T-10-5, T-10-6, T-10-9, T-10-10 and T-10-11, were built at the Komsomolsk-on-Amur production plant. From the third prototype, T10-3, power switched to the more powerful (in afterburner thrust) AL-31F turbofan engine developed to power the series production aircraft. Normal thrust ratings for this engine were given as 79.43 kN (17,857 lb.) dry and 122.59 kN (27,558 lb.) with afterburner. Available information indicates that the AL-31F has a nine-stage HP (High-Pressure) compressor, a four-stage LP (Low-Pressure) compressor and cooled single-stage HP and LP turbines to the rear of the combustor. The efficient air flow afforded by the combination of engine technology, the aircraft air intake design and computer controlled variable inlet guide-vanes, contributed to the Su-27 high performance, conveying varying degrees of capability to conduct extreme high alpha manoeuvres like the 'Cobra' or Tail Slide, without the engines stalling.

A Su-27S, Blue 388, lands at RAF Leuchars, Fife, Scotland, in September 1992. Author

When it entered service in the 1980's, the high thrust to weight ratio of the AL-31F bestowed upon the standard Su-27S a high maximum speed, unrivalled (for the time) supersonic acceleration, climb rate, and manoeuvrability, in certain flight regimes such as sustained turn rate, for an aircraft in its class. Typical engine life was set at around 3,000 hours with a TBO (Time Between Overhaul) of 1,000 hours; reasonable figures for a Soviet era fighter aircraft engine. It should be noted that AL-31F engines have been run for thousands of hours over their scheduled life expectancy during bench running tests.

A number of problems with performance goals were encountered during the T-10 flight test program resulting in the decision to implement a more or less complete redesign of the aircraft to address issues such as controlling weight, reducing drag, increase wing lift and improving roll control. The T-10-7 was therefore built as the prototype of the new design, receiving the new designation T-10S-1, which in turn received the NATO reporting name 'Flanker' B; the original T-10 aircraft having been allocated the NATO reporting name 'Flanker' A. The T-10S-1, which was more or less a new fighter aircraft design, was flown for the first time on 20 April 1981, the pilot being V.S. Ilyushin.

The Cold War ending, Su-27's were taken on tours of Europe and North America, allowing the designs manoeuvrability to be demonstrated to western observers, to a certain degree. US DoD

The T-10S-1 had a new tapered wing with a straight, slatted leading edge flap, flaperon and cropped wingtips incorporating missile launch rails that doubled as anti-flutter weights. The flaperons and differential tailerons replaced the ailerons of the original T-10 design. It was the changes to the fuselage that were most noticeable, with a shallower, longer drooping nose and deeper spine. The twin vertical tail fin configuration of the T-10 was retained, but this was moved outboard from the original position on top of the engine nacelles to booms, which lay alongside the engines. The main undercarriage door mounted air brakes of the T-10 were replaced by a single spine mounted unit similar to that seen on the F-15 Eagle. The new main undercarriage was repositioned, as was the nose wheel, which was moved aft.

When the T-10S-1, formerly the incomplete T-10-7, conducted its maiden flight in April 1981, it was clear that it was a new design. However, even with this new design, problems were encountered during flight testing, especially with the wing. The solution to this problem was to reduce the area of the leading-edge slats.

The new design that would evolve into the production Su-27S was equipped with a modern weapons system based around the RLPK-27 weapon control system, featuring a powerful N001 pulse-Doppler radar that was allocated the NATO reporting name 'Slot Back'. This system had a reported detection range of around 240 km, although manufacturer, Tikhomirov NIIP, information suggests 150 km against a fighter size target. The radar can track ten targets simultaneously, but once locked onto a target it could not continue to scan for others. The N001 radar was complemented by an electro-optical complex consisting of an OEPS-27 Electro-Optical Sighting System; an OLS-27 Optical Location System - IRST (Infra-Red Search and Track) and LR (Laser Rangefinder), allowing the detection, tracking and engagement of targets passively without the need for radar, the emissions of which can betray the host aircraft position. A Shchel helmet mounted target designation system allowed engagements of off-boresight targets up to 60° by cueing sensors - the missile tracker head - onto targets that had not been bore-sighted.

Once the design of the new fighter was finalised the Su-27S entered production (the first series production Su-27S conducted its maiden flight on 1 June 1982, piloted by Sukhoi test pilot A.N. Isakov) and entered service in June 1985, apparently with the 60th IAP-PVO (FAR). Although having been in service for over five years the Su-27 was officially signed into service by a decree of the Soviet government on 23 August 1990.

Although being partially replaced by Su-27SM3, Su-35S and Su-30SM multirole fighters, the baseline Su-27S, in early 2016, remains in widespread service with the Russian Federation Air Force and shore based naval aviation. This Su-27 was encountered by RAF Eurofighter Typhoons over the Baltic Sea in 2015. Crown Copyright

Despite the preponderance of twin-seat Su-27UB, Su30MKI and Su-30MKK deliveries in the first decade of the 21st century, the Sun had certainly not set on the single-seat advanced derivatives of the Su-27. Twelve new build Su-27SM3 multi-role fighters (top) were delivered to the Russian Federation Air Force from 2011, these being followed by the Su-35S 4++ generation super-manoeuvrable fighter (above) which entered Russian Federation Air Force service in 2014. Sukhoi

The Su-27UB operational conversion trainer introduced a second, slightly raised cockpit. Other than heightened tail fins, overall dimensions remained the same as those of the Su-27S, but maximum take-off weight was increased from 30450 kg to 33000 kg, which combined with increased drag, slightly degraded overall performance. Author

Su-27S series production aircraft, which are powered by a pair of AL-31F turbofan engines, each rated at 79.43 kN dry and 122.58 kN with afterburner, have a length of 21.9 m, height 5.9 m and wingspan 14.70 m. Normal take-off weight was set at 23400 kg (Su-27SK) with 2 x R-27R1 (NATO reporting name AA-10 'Alamo'), 2 x R-73 (NATO reporting name AA-11 'Archer') air to air missiles and 5270 kg of fuel. Maximum take-off weight is 30450 kg (Su-27SK). The Su-27 carries 5270 kg of fuel at normal load and 9400 kg at maximum fuel-load. The huge volume of fuel allowed an impressive range to be attained; the aircraft being capable of flying 1340 km at sea level armed with 2 x R-27R1 and 2 x R-73 missiles. In the same configuration, range is 3530 km at altitude. Payload, which can be carried on ten wing and fuselage stations, is, according to manufacturer information, 4430 kg, which can include the primary armament of R-27 semi-active radar homing and infrared homing air to air missile variants, and R-73 infrared guided air to air missiles, as well as unguided air to surface munitions for the secondary air to surface role.

Although a large heavy fighter, the Su-27 showed itself to have an exceptional performance, in many areas, such as range, climb rate, manoeuvrability, in particular its high alpha flight performance, being superior to its rivals. The airframe has a +9 g limit that can be over-ridden by switching the limiter off. Maximum level speed is stated as 1400 km/h at sea level and Mach 2.35 at altitude; climb rate is stated as 19800 meters per minute at sea level, with an operational ceiling of 18500 m.

Top and above: The Su-27, in both single-seat and two-seat variants, has been the mount of the Russian Knights aerobatics display team since its formation in 1991. Sukhoi/UAC

Following its introduction to service with the air forces of the Soviet Union in June 1985, production continued, with in excess of 500 Su-27's thought to have been produced by the time the Soviet Union began to crumble towards the end of 1991. Following the break-up of the Soviet Union in December 1991, the Su-27 remained in service in Russia, assuming greater importance as older aircraft were retired. It is estimated that around 300 Su-27's remain in service with Russia. Smaller numbers of Su-27's equipped the air forces of some former Soviet Republics and new build aircraft were exported to China, Vietnam and Indonesia, while surplus Russian and former Soviet Republics aircraft were exported to several other nations.

Other variants developed from the basic Su-27S included the naval Su-27K (officially designated Su-33 in 1998), and the Su-27M (original Su-35). Development work conducted for these variants, particularly in regards to the introduction of the canard tri-plane configuration, would be carried over to later advanced Su-27 derivatives including the side-by-side Su-34 strike aircraft, and of course the multi-role Su-30MKI family.

The two-seat Su-27 met with moderate export success, China being the major purchaser with several batches of Su-27UBK's, the last of which were delivered in 2002. US DoD

Like most single-seat tactical combat aircraft of its era a two-seat operational conversion trainer variant of the Su-27 was developed to ease the conversion of pilots onto the new fighter; development of this variant commencing in 1976. Designated T-10U-1, the prototype two-seat operational conversion trainer, known in service as the Su-27UB, was based on the production version of the single seat Su-27S. The main external differences were a redesigned forward fuselage incorporating a second cockpit that was raised above the front cockpit, affording a better forward view for the occupant in the rear cockpit. A single piece canopy covers the twin-cockpit, with a one-piece windscreen ahead of the front cockpit. The vertical tail planes and air brake were of increased height and area; the Su-27UB standing 500 mm taller than the Su-27S. Compared to the Su-27S, maximum take-off weight was increased from 30450 kg to 33000 kg, which, along with the extra drag caused by incorporation of the second cockpit, resulted in the overall performance being somewhat degraded compared to the Su-27S; maximum speed being reduced from Mach 2.35 to Mach 2.0 at altitude. Range was also reduced from 1340 km to 1270 km at sea level and from 3530 km to 3000 km at altitude. There was only a slight degradation in turn rates, initial climb rates and take-off and landing performance.

The first flight of the prototype, T-10U-1, took place on 7 March 1984, and the first series production Su-27UB, which was allocated the NATO reporting name 'Flanker' C, conducted its maiden flight on 10 September 1986, with deliveries commencing in 1987.

The prototype of the T-10PU (Su-30) design, T-10PU-5, could clearly be distinguished from the T-10U (Su-27UB) by the retractable in-flight refuelling probe located on the port side forward fuselage just forward of the windscreen. As with the Su-27K naval fighter, the addition of the refuelling probe required the OLS sensor, which on the Su-27S was centred ahead of the windscreen, to be offset to starboard. Sukhoi

Development of the Su-27UB paved the way for development of a new two-seat combat aircraft design commencing with an IA-PVO requirement for an interceptor capable of flying long duration patrols over the Soviet Union's vast land borders and coastline, as well as conducting offshore operations to provide air cover for naval forces. This program to field a low cost, low risk interceptor would sow the seeds for the later Su-30MK multi-role combat aircraft that would become a major success in both the export and domestic Russian markets.

The prototype T-10PU (Su-30), T-10PU-1, Blue 05, taxiing to or from dispersal during the flight test program around 1989-91. Much of the test program centred on new systems and flight profiles, much of the aerodynamic and stability and control testing having been conducted under the T-10U (Su-27UB) test program. Sukhoi

The design of a two-seat long-range interceptor development of the Su-27UB was initiated in the mid-1980's, around the same time that the operational conversion trainer variant went into production. The new interceptor, which was designated T-10PU (referred to as the Su-27PU/Su-30), appeared to differ very little in outward appearance to the Su-27UB when it was publically unveiled in the early 1990's; the most obvious differences being the incorporation of a retractable in-flight refuelling probe on the port side forward fuselage just forward of the windscreen, which, as first noted on the Su-27K, necessitated having the OLS-27 sensor, which on the Su-27S was centred ahead of the windscreen, offset to starboard. As was the case with the T-10UB (Su-27UB), the airframe of the T-10PU (Su-30) was constructed primarily of strengthened aluminium alloys and titanium. However, an undisclosed percentage of the airframe was constructed using composite materials, although this would have been small in area.

The T-10PU prototypes featured a modified FBW flight control system and enhancements to the avionics and fire control system, apparently including twin target engagement capability for the N001 radar, which was otherwise the same as the system installed in the Su-27S/UB; the radar system being complemented by the OEPS-27 combined IRST/LR as was the case with the Su-27UB.

Series production Su-30M, Blue 51, of the Russian Federation Air Force. Sukhoi

The high power of the N001 radar facilitated the requirement for the aircraft to be capable of operating in an ersatz mini-AWACS (Airborne Warning and Control System)/command post role, during which the aircraft would operate in conjunction with up to four other interceptors such as the Su-27S or other Su-30s, which could be automatically controlled and directed to targets in order of priority, whilst also receiving and transferring various data such as radar and other sensor inputs within the formation via a datalink. For such operations a fighter controller would have been carried in the rear cockpit, as was the case with the MiG-31 'Foxhound' long-range interceptor that pioneered this type of operation.

Among the systems incorporated into the design was a new navigation system developed by RPBK Ramenskoye, which combined laser-gyro inertial sensors with the GLONASS (Globanaya Navigozionnaya Sputnikovaya Sistema - Global Navigation Satellite System) and Loran.

Powerplant, fuel load and weapons load remained the same as those of the Su-27UB. In Russian service primary armament was to be the R-27R1 semi-active radar homing, R-27T1 infrared homing and R-73E short-range infrared guided air to air missiles. Later extended range ER1 and ET1 variants of the R-27 would be incorporated into the armoury.

Being almost aerodynamically identical to the Su-27UB, the overall performance of the T-10PU was more or less identical to the former design, with the exception of range/duration, which could be increased courtesy of the above mentioned in-flight refuelling capability. When the requirement for the new interceptor was being drawn up one of the primary stipulations was a ten hour endurance requiring the aircraft to have two pilots in duel cockpits so either of the pilots could take control of the aircraft at any given time during the mission.

The two prototypes, T-10PU-5 and T-10PU-6, coded Blue 05 and Blue 06 respectively, were converted from a pair of production standard Su-27UB operational conversion trainers, with conversion being completed around summer 1988; the Sukhoi in house designation was apparently Izdeiye 10-4-PU. The first of the prototypes, T-10PU-5, was flown for the first time, post conversion, from Sukhoi's Irkutsk plant in Southern Russia on 30 December 1989. Following a program of preliminary flight testing, T-10PU-5 and T-10PU-6 were transferred to the LLI test centre for further testing, following which the design was cleared for production with the service designation Su-30M.

Early operational tests showed that the aircraft had a range in excess of 3000 km, and this could be further increased with in-flight refuelling, making the aircraft ideal for operations in the vast expanse of Northern Russia where radar coverage is poor and often extremely adverse weather conditions made navigation difficult. As noted above, the PVO had stipulated a requirement for an aircraft with a ten hour endurance, this capability being aptly demonstrated on 6 June 1992, when a Su-30 was flown to the area of the North Pole and back in a time of 12 hours, employing three separate in-flight refuelling top-up's.

Conceived and built at a time when the Soviet Union was entering a tumultuous phase of political and financial instability, ultimately leading to its collapse and disintegration in December 1991, the Su-30's prospects for large scale production seemed bleak at best. As existing aircraft projects were being starved of funds Sukhoi stressed the in-house service designation of Su-30, indicating that it was a new program, in order to try to secure continued state funding for the project. The two T-10PU prototypes were followed by a small batch of production aircraft for operational service and a further two built for the Jupiter Insurance Company, both of which were operated alongside a single Su-27P with the Test Pilots display team based at the Gromov Flight Research Centre. These two aircraft were apparently the first two series production Su-30M, despite their Su-27PU designation. The aircraft, which were deficient of operational mission equipment, were coded White 596 and White 597 when they flew their public display debut at the MosAeroShow in August 1992.

By early 1996, around three Su-30M's were thought to have been delivered to the PVO's Savotsleyka air base near Nizhniy Novgorod; one of the Russian Federation Air Forces main advanced training bases. The Irkutsk plant was thought to have assembled up to thirty Su-30M's for the Russian Federation Air Force by 1997, and at the Mosero air show in 1999, Sukhoi exhibited a new Su-30M, indicating that production was continuing, however, available evidence indicates that deliveries to the Russian Federation Air Force were limited to the aforementioned three production aircraft, although the exact numbers of Su-30M's actually built is hard to accurately determine. The main operator of the Su-30M was apparently the IA-PVO's 148th Operational Conversion Unit (TsBP I PLS) combat conversion training unit based at Savotsleyka air base.

As the small number of Su-30M's began establishing themselves in the Russian Federation Air Force in the mid-to-late 1990's, a number of training exercises were conducted with other airborne assets, including the large Mach 2.83 capable MiG-31 'Foxhound' long-range interceptor, with mission durations of up to 10 hours being flown. Tactics employed during these joint training operations required the MiG-31's to fly ahead of the Su-30's using their more powerful N007 'Zaslon' phased-array radar to detect targets, apparently at ranges out to 200 km, the target information then being passed to the Su-30M's flying some 50-60 km behind the MiG-31's. These missions could cover vast areas of territory with distances of around 8000 km being flown, requiring the use of in-flight refuelling aircraft, which were typically Ilyushin Il-76 airborne tankers. The operations were also supported by Ilyushin E-50 AWACS aircraft.

The Su-30KN (above) upgrade program was designed to introduce a true multi-role capability to Su-30M class aircraft, however, the program would eventually be overshadowed by the Russian Federation Air Force drive to introduce a series of 4+/4++ generation multi-role fighters aircraft leading to service entry of the Su-35S and Su-30SM super manoeuvrable fighters in the second decade of the 21st century.
Irkut Corporation

Russia embarked upon an upgrade program for its Su-30M interceptor fleet under the initial designation Su-30KN. This added an enhanced air to surface capability with advanced precision guided munitions, and the aircraft was to be capable of operating with the Vympel (JSC Tactical Missiles Corporation) RVV-AE active radar guided medium range air to air missile, but the importance of this program waned with few implementations as a new generation of advanced Sukhoi fighters, Su-35S and Su-30SM were procured.

2

SU-30MK DEMONSTRATOR AND SU-30K INTERIM EXPORT FIGHTER

With the Soviet Union/Russia's economic plight in the early 1990's ruling out any large production run for domestic use the export market was seen as the best prospect for the Su-30. However, if the Su-30 was going to have any realistic chance of being an export success it was clear that additional multirole capability would have to be incorporated into the design as few nations would be in the market for a dedicated long-range interceptor in the class of the Su-30M.

The new multirole export variant emerged as the Su-30MK, which was first promulgated under Soviet leadership in 1991, although detailed design work was not initiated until late 1992/early 1993. Certainly in regards to the fire control system and elements of the avionics suite, design of the Su-30MK would capitalise on work being conducted on the Su-27M advanced single-seat evolution of the Su-27S. In particular the Tikhomirov Bars radar system was coveted for inclusion in the Su-30MK, replacing the same designers N001 system installed in the Su-27 and Su-30M long-range interceptor. The Bars system would bestow a proficient multirole capability upon the Su-30MK, allowing the engagement of ground and sea surface targets with a wide-range of precision guided air to ground and anti-ship weapons. Air to air capability would be significantly enhanced by the Bars systems greater performance parameters and operating modes, combined with the addition of the RVV-AE active radar guided medium range air to air missile.

The Su-30MK weighed in at around 34000 kg at maximum take-off weight; 1000 kg heavier than the standard Su-27UB at maximum take-off weight, depending on equipment fit. In the new multirole combat aircraft the back seat occupant was to be a weapons system operator, supervising target selection and weapon delivery as well as overseeing operation of other functions of the weapons control system. The aircraft featured an in-flight refuelling probe located on the port side forward fuselage just below and slightly ahead of the cockpit. Unlike series production Su-30 variants, the Su-30MK demonstrator featured a single nose-wheel undercarriage unit similar to that installed on the Su-27UB.

Resplendent in a multi-tone desert environment camouflage scheme, the Su-30MK Demonstrator, side code 603, lines up for take-off at the Farnborough International Trade Show in September 1996. Author

Details for the early Su-30MK developments are a little sketchy, even official information sources contradict each other as to timeframes and aircraft involved. It seems that when preliminary design of the multirole variant was initiated in 1991, in order to flight test some systems for the projected Su-30MK, modification work was authorized on Su-27UB Blue 389, serial: 96310413042, which was then recoded 321, although this aircraft was still designated Su-27UB with the side code Blue 389 when it visited Scotland in September 1992. Another aircraft, Su-30M Blue 56, was also modified to test elements of the new design. These aircraft would allow elements of the flight test program to commence whilst the Su-30MK demonstrator was being prepared, this aircraft, serial: 79371010101, emerging in 1993 with the side code Outline 603.

In June 1993, masquerading as a Su-30MK, the modified Su-27UB, side code 321, participated in the 40th Paris Air Salon at Le Bourget airport. This aircraft lacked such modifications as an inflight-refuelling probe, being, as noted above, little more than an Su-27UB dressed as the new multirole Su-30MK, exhibited with a number of precision guided weapon mockups. Still masquerading as an Su-30MK, Su-27UB, side code 321, was displayed in the static park at Russia's premier domestic air event, MAKS, held at Zhukovsky from the last day of August until 5 September 1993, the aircraft also being displayed at IDEX 93 in Dubai, UAE (United Arab Emirates).

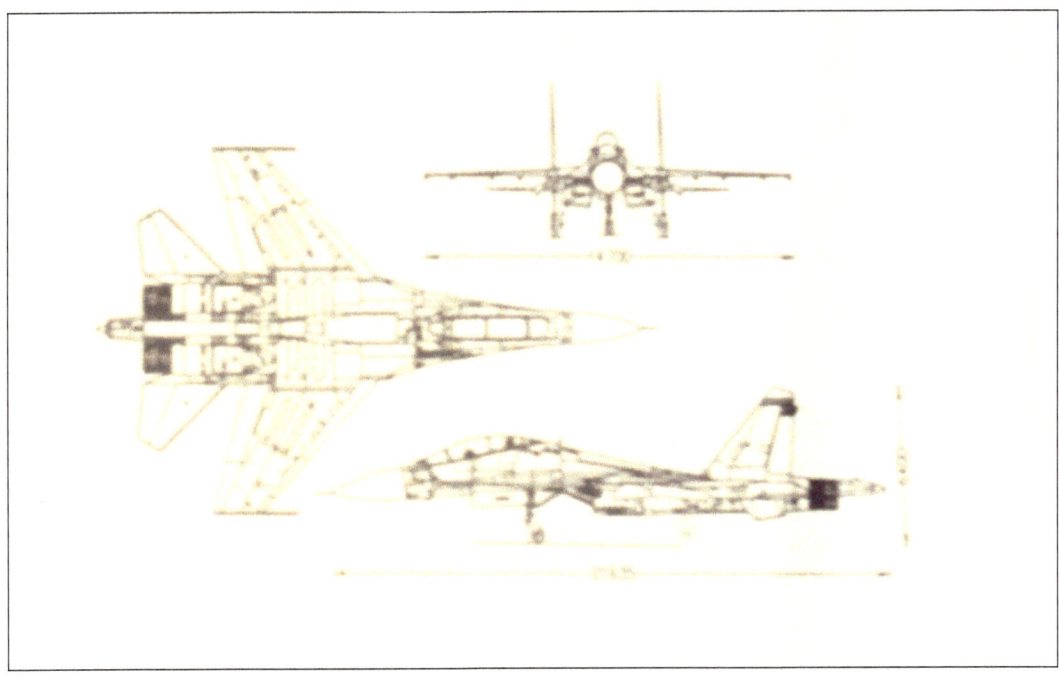

Top: Su-27UB, Blue 389, was still coded as such in mid-September 1992, as evidenced by its presence at RAF Leuchars, Fife, Scotland, where it is here shown alongside a RAF McDonnel Douglas Phantom FGR.2 which was on the cusp of retirement from operational service. Author

Above: **General arrangement of the Su-30MK as depicted by Sukhoi in 1996.** Author

Aerodynamically and structurally the Su-30MK appeared identical to the Su-30M. Author

Previous page top: Like the Su-30M, the Su-30MK could be distinguished from the Su-27UB by the addition of a retractable in-flight refueling probe located on the port side forward fuselage necessitating the OLS sensor ball being offset to starboard. Previous page bottom and this page top: Su-30MK, Outline 603, engages afterburner at the start of its take-off roll at Farnborough 1996. Above: With spine mounted airbrake deployed, Su-30MK, 603, lands at Farnborough in September 1996. Author.

The Su-30MK, above, would soon be overshadowed by the Su-30MKI, the first of the so called 'super-manoeuvrable' variants, although all Su-30 export variants, including the Su-30MKK/MK2, non-canard triplane/thrust vector control family built at KnAAPO would all be referred to under the 'MK' label by Sukhoi JSC. Author

Flight testing of the baseline Su-30MK demonstrator, Outline 603, was completed in 1993, and the design was officially offered on the export market from 1993/94, the first real interest in the aircraft being expressed by India in the latter year; a year in which outline 603 was exhibited in a number of foreign and domestic air events such as FIDEA 94 in Santiago, Chile, the aircraft conducting an unrefueled crossing of the Atlantic Ocean on its journey to that country. In early summer 1994, the aircraft was displayed at ILA 94 in Berlin before being displayed at Farnborough, United Kingdom, in September that year. Highlights for 1995 included participation in shows in China, India and Malaysia as well as the domestic MAKS show at Zhukovsky.

In order to facilitate early deliveries an interim export variant, the T-10-4PK, with the service designation Su-30K, was offered to potential customers while the Su-30MK was undergoing detailed development. The Su-30K was basically a standard Su-30M interceptor with slight changes to some systems, including the IFF (Identification Friend or Foe), and the communications and navigation suite, retaining the export version of the Tikhomirov NIIP N001 radar, and powered by the standard AL-31F engines of the Su-30M.

Previous page top: A pair of Indian Air Force Su-30K's flank a pair of USAF F-15 fighters, with a pair of IAF Mirage 2000's in the van, during exercise Cope India. Previous page bottom: IAF Su-30K, SB 010, from the second batch of 10 aircraft, lands during a stopover en-route to the USA. USAF

This page top: A Su-30K armed with R-27 and R-73E air to air missiles and empty multiple-ejector racks for unguided air to surface munitions. Above: A Su-30K flanked by an IAF MiG-29 and SEPECAT Jaguar international strike aircraft. IAF

In July 1996, India ordered an initial batch of eight Su-30K's from an initial requirement for forty Su-30's for service with the IAF (Indian Air Force). The remaining 32 aircraft were to be ordered to a more advanced multi-role standard, which was still being defined in summer 1996; this order being placed in November that year. This second batch was to be equipped with thrust-vectoring equipped AL-31FP (initially reported as FU) engines, Tikhomirov NIIP N011M 'Bars' phased-array radar and an advanced flight-control system, with these features to potentially be retrofitted to the Su-30K aircraft at a later date. Included in the $1.2 billion sale for the forty aircraft, eight Su-30K and 32 Su-30MK (later known as the Su-30MKI), was associated weapons and a production licence for India to build 100+ aircraft.

Su-30K, SB 006, from the IAF No.24 'Hawks' Squadron. IAF

Due to delays to the initial planned in service date for the Su-30MKI, India signed a $300 million contract for an additional ten Su-30K's to supplement the eight Su-30K's ordered in July 1996, to which standard they would equate.

As the IAF prepared for its Su-30K's, air and ground personnel began training at Zhukovsky in January 1997. The first two Su-30K's for the IAF were delivered to Lohegaon air base near Pune as air freight inside a Russian Antonov An-124 'Ruslan' transport aircraft on 19 March 1997. Another two aircraft were delivered to Pune on 26 March, followed by two more on 9 April; the last two of the initial batch of eight aircraft, which had been allocated serials SB001 to SB008, being delivered on 15 April 1997. The second batch of ten Su-30K's were allocated the serials SB 009 to SB 018.

The Su-30K officially entered service with the IAF during a ceremony at Lohegaon air base on 11 June 1997, with the Poona based No.24 'Hawks' Squadron being the first IAF squadron to equip with the type. Following a short work-up training period, three No.24 Squadron Su-30K's participated in exercise 'Vaga Shakti 1998', which commenced on 22 March that year. This exercise saw the aircraft employed primarily as an air to ground platform using unguided munitions. India took delivery of all eighteen Su-30K's before the end of 1999, allowing a full established squadron to be maintained until the aircraft were withdrawn around 2006/7 as deliveries of the Su-30MKI ramped up.

3

SU-30MK SUPER MANOEUVRABLE FAMILY – SU-30MKI/SU-30MKM/SU-30MKI(A)

By the time India had ordered its first batch of Su-30K's in July 1996, Sukhoi had begun pushing a canard foreplane, thrust vector nozzle control variant of the Su-30, development of which had commenced a year or so earlier under the leadership of Sukhoi Design Bureau, with production assigned to IAPA (Irkut Aircraft production Association - now Irkut Corporation) in co-operation with Saturn, RPKB, Tikhomirov NIIP and a number of other Russian and international companies; India quickly expressing interest in this more advanced combat aircraft.

The 'canard-tri-plane' configuration, which retains the rear all-moving horizontal tail planes, but adds all-moving active canard foreplanes just ahead of the main wing where the fuselage and wing join, had been developed in the 1980's for the T-10K (Su-27K) naval variant of the T-10S (Su-27S); the all-moving canards being flight-tested on the T-10-24, the first Su-27 variant to be flown with canard foreplanes, which were being studied by Sukhoi as a means of increasing the Su-27s take-off performance and approach speed as well as increasing the designs already impressive manoeuvrability.

Studies of a canard equipped variant of the T-10 commenced around 1977, and the maiden flight of the T-10-24 equipped with canards took place in May 1985, by which time the aircraft had also been fitted with production standard vertical tail fins featuring the cropped fin tip. The T-10-24 was followed by a prototype of the Su-27K naval fighter, T-10K-1 (also known as the T-10-37, the latter figure denoting the aircraft side code), built in 1986-87, which was fitted with canard foreplanes that could deflect +7° to -70°.

Although initially associated with the Su-27K, the T-10-24 was effectively used to prove the capability of the canards for all the canard tri-plane equipped members of the Su-27 family, including the Su-27M, Su-27IB (Su-34), Su-27KUB and the Su-30MKI/SM family, all of which, unlike the Su-27K, featured digital FBW (Fly-By-Wire) FCS (Flight Control Systems).

Irkut Corporation operates a small fleet of Su-30MKI development aircraft, some of which were also used in the development programs for the Su-30MKM/MKI(A) and the domestic Su-30SM(CM). JSC Corporation Irkut

While the first generations of the Su-27 family were highly manoeuvrable, certainly surpassing their western rivals in most areas, it was with Su-27M, tail code 711, which carried the Sukhoi designation Su-37MR, that led to a significant further advance in high alpha capability that would eventually result in the 21st century 'super-manoeuvrable' fighters of the Su-30MKI and Su-35S multirole fighter families equipped with thrust vector control for the engine nozzles and, in the case of the Su-30MKI family, active canard foreplanes.

The main aim of the Su-27M program had been to introduce to the Su-27 more modern avionics and fire control systems, greater air to surface capability and enhanced agility, particularly in the slow speed high alpha flight regime. Enhanced agility and better control and handling characteristics were achieved through the introduction of forward canard foreplanes like those on the Su-27K, combined with a new quadruplex FBW FCS. While the first generation Su-27S used FBW control in pitch only, the Su-27M introduced FBW control in all axes, with four longitudinal channels in pitch (up/down) and three in roll/yaw (port/starboard), paving the way for the advanced FCS's installed in the Su-30MKI family. To compensate for the effect of the canards the vertical tail area was increased on some of the Su-27M development aircraft; the new tail fins being similar to the increased height vertical tail introduced with the Su-27UB, but with the rudder extended downward to the fin base and the fin tops squared off; the tail fin of the Su-30 being considered aerodynamically efficient when accounting for the forces exerted by the canards.

The canard-foreplane configuration adopted by the Su-30MKI had previously been tried and tested on a number of Su-27 derivatives, including the Su-27K (top) and the Su-34 (above). Sukhoi/UAC

The Su-37MR demonstrator, seen here at Farnborough in September 1996, was the first of the canard-triplane Su-27 derivatives to be equipped with thrust vector control for the engine nozzles. Author

With the canard-triplane Su-27M program stuck in the quagmire that was the funding drought in the mid-1990's, Sukhoi continued to refine the design which culminated in the Su-37MR (the 11th Su-27M development aircraft, tail code 711, equipped with a thrust-vector control system for the AL-31F derivative engines.

The Su-37MR, which can claim to be the first of the super-manoeuvrable Su-27 derivatives, appears to have flown in 1996, a series of flights being conducted out of Zhukovsky. The aircraft made its public debut at the Tushino Air Fleet Day where it conducted a series of spectacular manoeuvres including a rapid pitch upwards following which the aircraft recovered in an inverted posture before it continued into what could be described as a half loop to bring it back into normal level flight, all conducted within a very small turn radius. A few weeks after the Tushino display, the aircraft was dispatched to the United Kingdom where it displayed at the Farnborough (Society of British Aerospace Companies) trade show, flying its first display there on 4 September 1996.

The Su-27M (including the Su-37MR) did feature a number of improvements in areas of avionics, power, range, agility and weapon delivery. However, in Russia's post-Cold War, post-communism economic downturn, no large domestic production orders were forthcoming and the aircraft attracted little export interest, the program being cancelled as export customers began looking to the two-seat Su-30 variants, which gained increasing success from designs produced at both KnAAPO (Komsomolsk-on-Amur Aircraft Production Association) and IAPA at Irkutsk.

The Su-30I-1 (Su-30MKI prototype) under conversion (top) and during its post conversion maiden flight (above) still adorned with its pre-conversion side code, **Blue 56.** Sukhoi

As the Su-30MKI was being developed, various models (code 01 of the first prototype top and code 06 of the second prototype bottom) were presented at trade shows such as the Paris Air Salon at Le Bourget airport and the Farnborough International Trade show in the United Kingdom. Author

Construction of a prototype canard equipped Su-30 was initiated at IAPA in 1995. This aircraft, which was a production standard Su-30M interceptor with side code Blue 56, was, post conversion, erroneously reported as carrying the designation Su-30I or Su-30I (Istrivitel\fighter), however, according to JSC Sukhoi and Irkut Corporation records the prototype was officially designated Su-30I-1, the in-house designation of T-10PMK-1 being allocated.

While the IAF (Indian Air Force) was taking delivery of its first Su-30K's Sukhoi was preparing the Su-30I-1 for its maiden flight, conversion work on the aircraft being completed in spring 1997, following which the aircraft was delivered to the LII facility at Zhukovsky on 23 April that year. Over the next several weeks the aircraft was put through a program of ground testing, including low and high speed taxi runs, in preparation for its post conversion maiden flight, which was conducted on 1 July 1997, with test pilot V. Yu. Averynov at the controls for the 50 minute flight. Following a handful of checkout flights the aircraft entered into a rigorous joint test program with Sukhoi and SPFC of the Russian Federation Air Force.

After initially flying as the Su-30I-1 with the Blue 56 code, the aircraft was eventually re-coded Blue 01, being universally referred to as the Su-30MKI prototype despite its official Su-30I-1 label; the Su-30MK badge was painted on the vertical tail fins; all variants of the Su-30MK retaining the MK designation at JSC Sukhoi regardless of whether they emanate from Irkut Corporation or KnAAPO where the less advanced Su-30MKK/MK2 family of multi-role strike fighters was developed.

The first development Su-30MKI, here armed with a load of unguided bombs, was re-coded Blue 01, a code it retained until it was lost in a crash at the Paris Air Salon in June 1999. Author

Previous page and above: The second Su-30MKI prototype, Blue 06, demonstrates the designs extreme high alpha capability in the low-speed flight regime. Sukhoi

The second prototype Su-30MKI was converted from the T-10PU-6, which was the sixth pre-production Su-27UB two-seat operational trainer variant of the Su-27. This aircraft received the designation T-10PMK-6 post conversion and was coded Blue 06. First flight as the T-10PMK-6 took place on 23 March 1998. This aircraft differed from the first Su-30MKI prototype, the Su-30I-1, in retaining the standard Su-27UB single wheel forward undercarriage unit, the first prototype and the production standard Su-30MKI having a twin nose-wheel unit.

The Su-30MKI had its public debut when Blue 01 was displayed at Tushino on 16 August 1998, followed by an appearance at Bangalore in India in November that year. Blue 01 was also displayed at Le Bourget, Paris, France, in June 1999, where it crashed during the first day of display.

As well as the two prototype Su-30MKI's, a small fleet of pre-production aircraft was built at the IAPA/Irkut Corporation Irkutsk aviation production facility to accelerate all aspects of flight development of, not only the Su-30MKI ordered for the Indian Air Force, but later variants, the Su-30MKM for Malaysia, the Su-30MKI(A) for Algeria and the domesticated Su-30SM(CM) built for Russia and exported to Kazakhstan.

Page 35-37: Su-30MKI pre-production aircraft Blue 04. Irkut Corporation/UAC

Su-30MKI pre-production aircraft side code 03 with the additional tail code 722 representing the last three digits of the serial number. Irkut Corporation

Changes to the Su-30MKI aerodynamic layout and control surfaces compared to the baseline Su-30MK demonstrator of 1993 included the addition of the canard-foreplanes and axisymmetric thrust vector control for the engine nozzles. UAC

The production variant ordered for the IAF, known as the T-10-4PMK2, with the service designation Su-30MKI, was the first serial produced combat aircraft featuring so called 'super manoeuvrability' – courtesy of the aerodynamic configuration and thrust vector control system for the AL-31FP engines; the Su-30MKI was also the first mass produced fighter aircraft intended for export equipped with a phased-array antenna. A true multirole weapon system, this advanced combat aircraft bestows upon the IAF improved capabilities in air superiority, ground strike and maritime surface strike capabilities, armed with a diversity of advanced air to air and air to surface precision guided and unguided weapons. Another role for the Su-30MKI would be a long range interceptor/controller capable of controlling the IAF upgraded RAC MiG-29UPG 'Fulcrum' and upgraded RAC MiG-21UPG 'Fishbed' multirole fighter aircraft in a similar fashion to that initially conducted by the Russian Su-30M, equipped with a data link for information transfer.

The basic aircraft aerodynamic design, lift-enhancing canard-tri-plane configuration - unstable in the longitudinal channel - electronic control system and thrust-vector control for the engine nozzles, all combine to ensure the Su-30MKI has greater manoeuvring capabilities than those of its rivals, particularly in the low speed high alpha - AoA (Angle-of-Attack) - flight regime. During flight the canards are deflected automatically by the digital Fly-By-Wire Flight Control System increasing aircraft performance at high AoA. These qualities translated to unrivalled high alpha manoeuvring capabilities until the advent of the Su-35S produced by KnAAPO at Komsomolsk-on-Amur; this latter design entering service with the Russian Federation Air Force in 2014.

Derived from the standard Su-27UB undercarriage units, the SU-30MKI system is strengthened to take increased weights, with a twin nose-wheel unit derived from that of the Su-27M. UAC/USAF

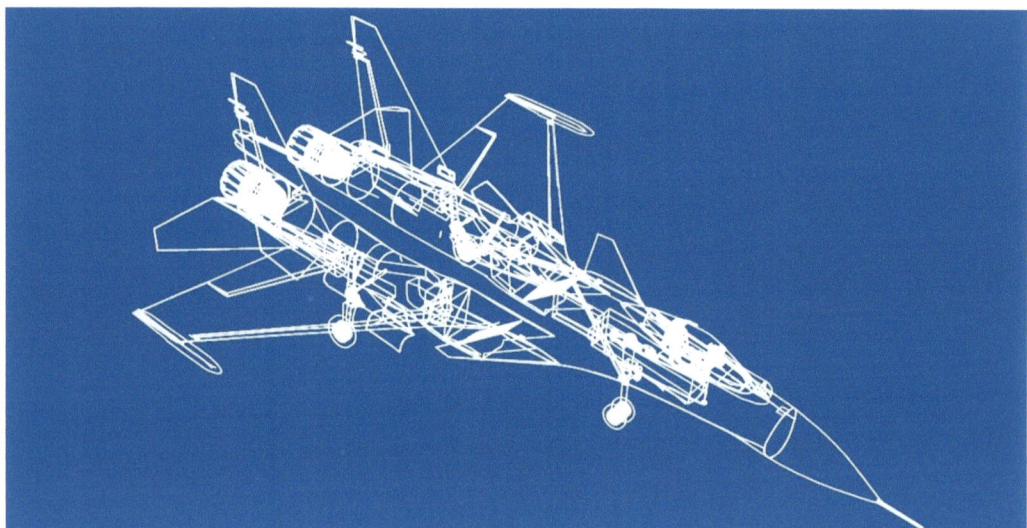

Top: Depiction of the Su-30MKI aerodynamic layout and control surfaces. Above: Ghosted view of a Su-30MKI derivative showing the internal layout of such systems as the engines. Note this depiction has squared off vertical tail tops as found on the Su-30MK2 family, whereas all members of the Su-30MKI family incorporate the sloped back vertical tail tops. UAC

The Su-30MKI family can operate in a number of automated flight modes, which, according to JSC Corporation Irkut, includes "low altitude, as well as individual or group combat employment against air, ground and sea targets". JSC Corporation Irkut continues, "The automatic control associated with the navigation system provides a cross-country flight, the approach to targets, return to the airfield and landing approach in automatic mode". The aircraft has full autopilot capability in all flight regimes including a terrain following mode for high-speed flight at low-altitude.

Manoeuvrability is further increased by the use of thrust-vector control in combination with the flight control system, bestowing upon the aircraft the ability to conduct a number of extreme manoeuvres that could not be emulated by any other in service combat aircraft until the advent of the Su-35S. Such manoeuvring capability significantly enhances the aircraft survivability, be it in close range combat with an enemy aircraft or in evading air to air missiles launched by an adversary. The incorporation of thrust vector control has other benefits, such as improved runway performance and increased aircraft safety, for example in prevention of spin stalling.

Performance figures for all Su-30 variants is generally in the same ball park, the major difference being the increased range of the KnAAPO built Su-30MKK/MK2, the first and second MKK prototypes shown above. As well as increased range, the Su-30MKK/MK2 series had slightly better values for kinetic performance, but lacked the so-called 'super-manoeuvrability' of the Su-30MKI series, although they still possessed the excellent agility inherent in the basic Su-27 design. UAC

The basic Su-30MKI design is 21.9 m in length, 6.4 m in height with a 14.7 m wingspan. Normal take-off weight is in the region of 24000 kg, maximum take-off weight is 34000 kg and maximum landing weight is 30000 kg. Internal fuel load is set at 5270 kg normal and 9400 kg maximum, although this latter value cannot be carried when the aircraft is operating at its maximum external stores load of 8000 kg, unlike the Su-30MK2 series which can operate at maximum fuel and maximum weapon load.

Range when operating with a maximum fuel load on an air defence mission in which 2 x R-27R1 and 2 x R-73E air to air missiles are expended "at half distance" is set at 1270 km at sea level and 3000 km at altitude, without employing in-flight refueling, and 5200 km with the addition of one in-flight refueling courtesy of the built-in retractable in-flight refueling probe located on the port forward fuselage just below and forward of the cockpit canopy. This system features an NPP Zvezda -1,-M, 1N nozzle assembly which allows fuel to be transferred in flight at a maximum flow rate of 1100 l/m at an entry pressure of 3.5 kg/cm^3. The universality of the system, development of which was completed in 2006, allows aircraft to be refueled by Russian and foreign, including NATO, refueling aircraft.

Ground operations performance includes a take-off run of 550 m at normal take-off weight and a landing roll of 750 m at normal landing weight when a brake parachute is deployed.

As with the Su-27UB, the Su-30 variants are encumbered with degraded kinetic performance compared to the single-seat variants of the Su-27, Su-33 and Su-35S. For the Su-30MKI series maximum level speed at sea level is set at 1350 km/h and 2100 km/h at altitude, the latter value corresponding to a Mach number in the region of 1.9. Operating ceiling is set at 17300 m.

The NPP Zvezda -1,-M,1N equips the Su-30MKI series allowing the aircraft to be refueled in-flight. The system comprises a refueling coupling, an engagement warning system, a pneumatic drive to open refueling valves of the nozzle assembly/refueling pod drogue, an output fuel pressure regulator, a structural fuse of the refueling coupling and an emergency retraction system for the refueling coupling. NPP Zvezda

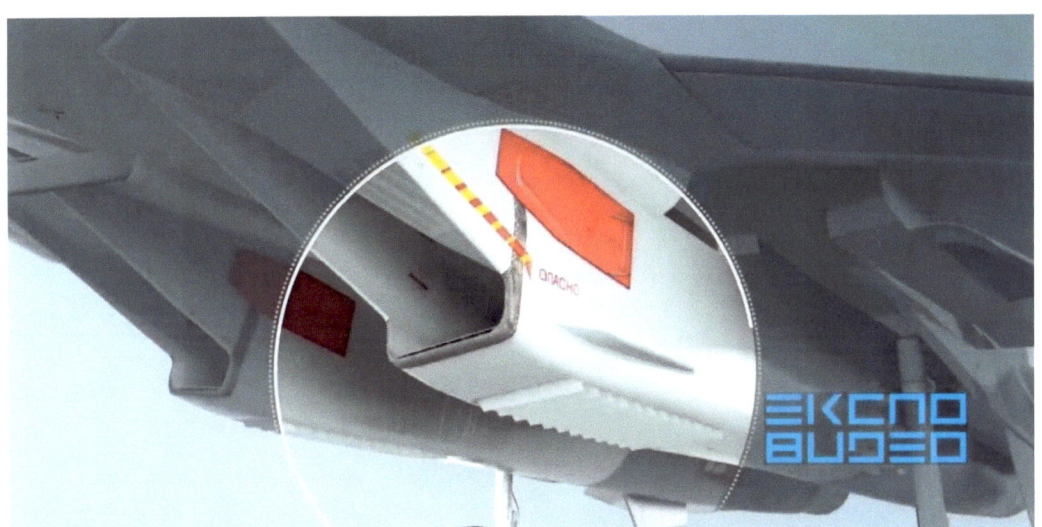

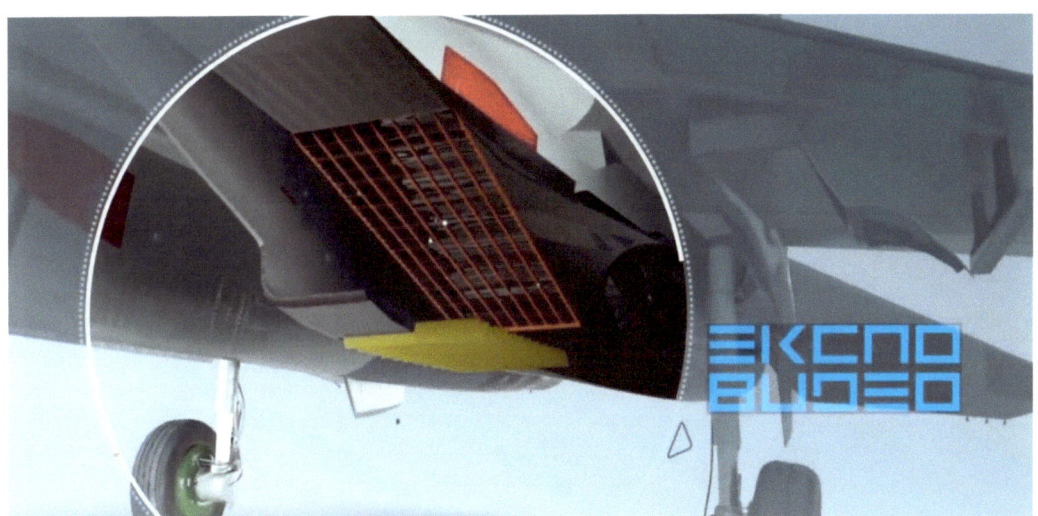

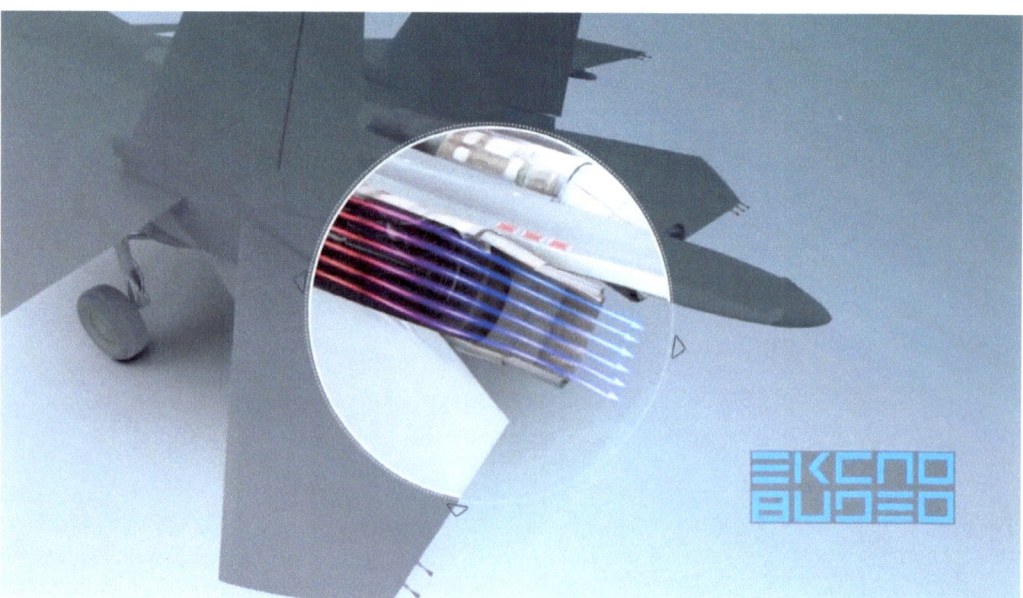

Previous page: While the Su-30 variants have degraded overall kinetic performance in comparison to the single-seat Su-27 and Su-35S variants, they retain the excellent high alpha characteristics. The upper graphic illustrates the efficient aerodynamic configuration of the air intake (top) allowing adequate supply of air to the engines even when performing extreme high alpha manoeuvres. The FOD (Foreign Object Damage) prevention grid is shown in place on the centre graphic and lowered for routine flight in the lower graphic. UAC

This page: Ghosted graphics showing the AL-31FP engine and nozzle arrangement (upper) and airflow (lower) on the Su-30MKI. UAC

The AL-31FP is a heavily modified derivative of the standard AL-31F engine incorporating the thrust-vector control system for the engine nozzles. Performance figures generally equate to those of the baseline AL-31F. NPO Saturn

Modifications to the basic Su-30MK structure included a strengthened and modified rear fuselage able to accommodate the AL-31FP with provision for axisymmetric thrust vectoring engine nozzles. The main changes to the AL-31FP, which is the standard powerplant of the Su-30MKI and its derivatives, are in relation to the associated thrust vector control system.

The T-10PMK-1 prototype was flown with a number of AL-31F derived engine variants. Initial flights were conducted with two engines initially referred to as AL-31FU (unofficial designation), each rated at 28,210 lb in afterburner and featuring pitch and yaw thrust vector control. These engines were replaced by two AL-31FP's following early flight testing, these it often being erroneously stated, featuring thrust vector control in pitch only with deflection angles up to $\pm15°$. Production standard engines certainly feature thrust vector control in pitch and yaw. The two axisymmetric thrust vector rotary nozzles have a differential deflection of up to $\pm15°$; the axis of rotation of each nozzle being arranged at an angle of 32° respective to each other, facilitating the employment of thrust vector control in both pitch and yaw axis. "Depending on the upcoming manoeuvre, the nozzles may vary in synchronism with horizontal tail assembly or separately from it", states JSC Corporation Irkut. The nozzle angling can apparently generate what is termed a 'side force' when differential deflection is selected, further increasing low speed manoeuvrability. A novel feature of the engine nozzles, which settle in the maximum downward position once the engines are shut-down, is that their movement is powered by the fuel system which reduces overall weight of the thrust vector control system whereas the convention for thrust vector control at the time of their design incorporated hydraulic control with the associated penalty of increased weight.

Current performance figures for the AL-31FP, which has a Length of 4.945 m and a dry weight of 1520 kg, are: 12500 kgf maximum thrust, 0.695 minimum fuel consumption kg/kgf/per hour and air consumption of 112 kg/s. The engine has a MTBO (Mean Time between Overhaul) of 1,000 hours, assigned life 2,000 hours and a thrust vector nozzle MTBO of 500 hours. Powered by two AL-31FP's the production standard Su-30MKI has a climb rate of 230 m/s and, as noted above, a maximum level speed at altitude of Mach 1.9.

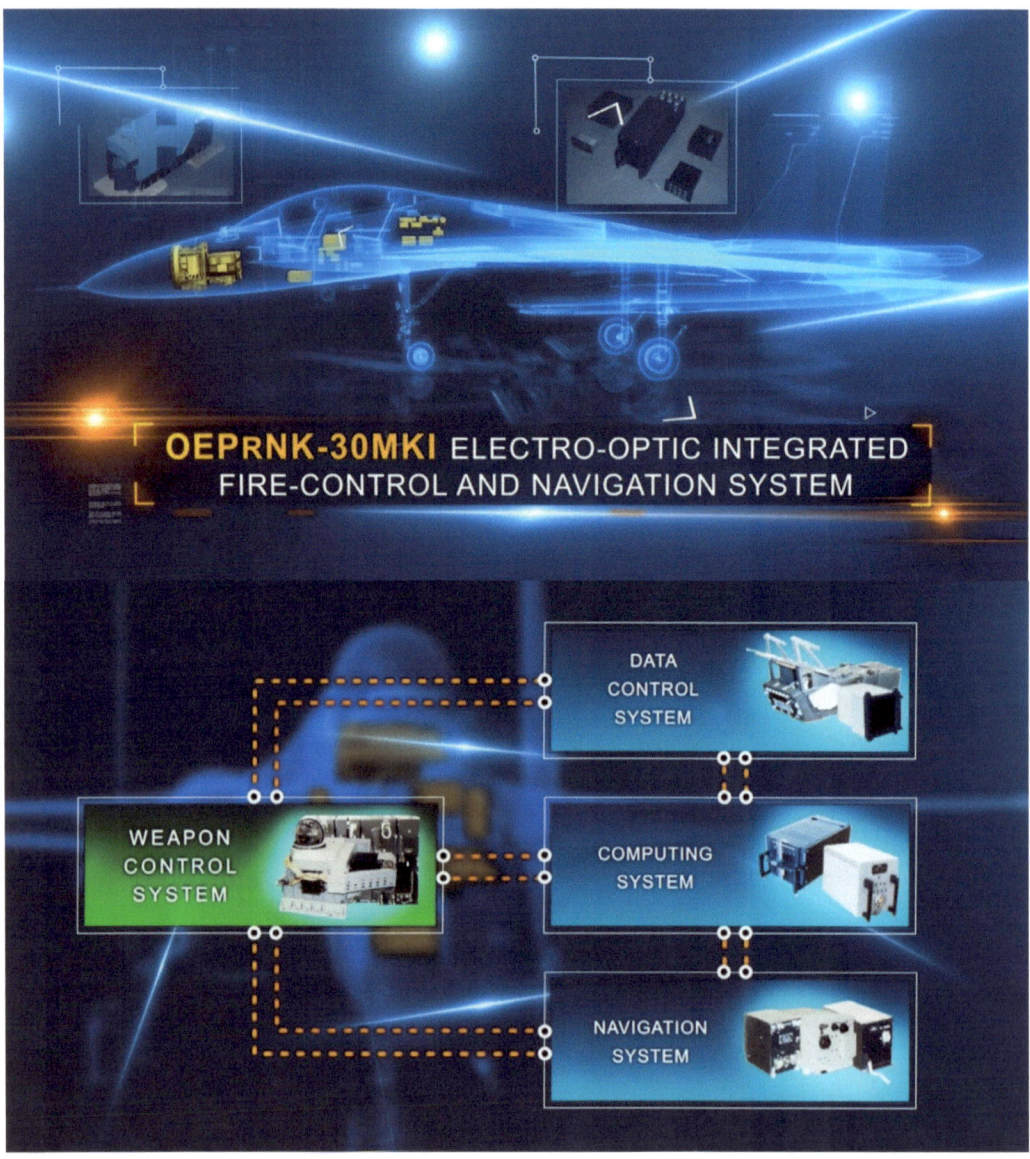

The Su-30MKI is equipped with the RPKB OEPrNK-30MKI Electro-Optic integrated fire control and navigation system, which integrates the aircraft fire control, data control, computing and navigation systems. RPKB

Designed for the Su-30MKI by RPKB Ramenskoye Design Bureau, the OEPrNK-30MKI – Electro-Optic Integrated Fire Control and Navigation System utilises open architecture technology to integrate a number of systems, including avionics, fire control and navigation, thus allowing ease of integration of new systems and weapons as technology advances. The OEPrNK-30MKI system comprises a triple-redundancy central digital computing system, navigation system, which relays coordinates and other data such as aircraft flight speed, data control system comprising the HUD (Heads Up Display), seven MFDS (Multi-Function Display Screens), data control panel and standby displays, and the Weapon Control System. The manufacturer states, "Target designation generates an electro-optic fire control system after primary processing is delivered to missile homing heads. The Integrated fire control system provides target lock-on, weapon selection and missile launch. Tasks are shared between two-crew members; example one member monitors airspace, the second monitors ground. The system components are designed in cooperation with companies from Russian, India, Ukraine, France and Israel.

The Su-30SM, developed for the Russian domestic market, is equipped with the OEPrNK-30SM, which replaces most foreign sourced components with Russian components, including updated fire control and navigation components, allowing the integration of new generation medium and long range missiles. As stated by RPKB, "The updated algorithms of group actions task for different types of aircraft is implemented in the suite."

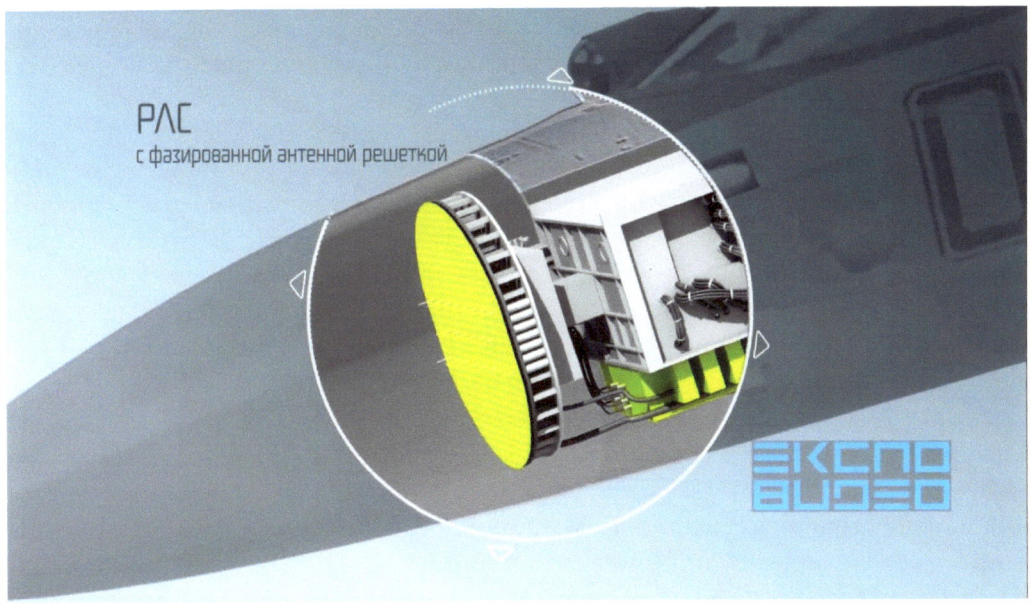

The primary sensor for all variants of the Su-30MK super-manoeuvrable series, the Su-30MKI, Su-30MKM, Su-30MKI(A) and the domestic Su-30SM(CM) is the V. Tikhomirov NIIP N011 Bars multi-mode radar system housed in the aircraft nose. This system replaces the less capable N001 system installed in the Su-27 and Su-30MKK/MK2 series. UAC

The Bars system has been operational on IAF Su-30MKI's since the first aircraft were delivered in 2002, progressively more capable sets being introduced as the program advanced. While the system installed in the Su-30MKI/MKM/MKI(A) are to more or less the same standard, the system installed in the domestic Su-30SM, apparently referred to as the Bars-R, incorporates a number of additional operating modes over the export models. JSC Corporation Irkut

At the heart of the Su-30MKI family capabilities is the V. Tikhomirov NIIP N011M Bars multi-mode radar system incorporating a phased-array antenna, apparently featuring mechanical and electronic beam steering. This system can simultaneously track up to 15 airborne targets and can simultaneously engage four whilst operating against ground clutter in a hostile jamming environment. The radar is also capable of a wide range of air to surface modes and can be used for high, medium and low resolution ground mapping.

Standard air to air modes include track while scan, velocity search, target identification and close range combat. Air-to-ground modes include Doppler beam sharpening mapping, real beam mapping, SAR (Synthetic Aperture Radar) mapping and moving ground target tracking. Maritime modes include surface search, moving target tracking, target identification and coordinates. The Bars radar system was gradually enhanced as the IAF received more capable variants of the Su-30MKI in varying phases of the acquisition program.

The N011M, which is around 1-metre in diameter, weights around 100 kg. India cooperates in the manufacture of the radar, supplying the radar controller. Other avionics systems supplied by India include the mission computer and display processor.

The following information on the Bars radar system has been furnished by the manufacturer, V. Tikhomirov NIIP.

Radar control system 'Bars' for Su-30MKI, Su-30MKI(A), Su-30MKM fighters

Multifunctional radar 'Bars' is intended for: Provision of data to the crew and weapon control system (WCS) on air and ground radiocontrast targets, their coordinates and characteristics, with accuracies required to make a decision on attack and carrying out the attack by means of weapons;

Provision of illumination and transmission of 'Air-to-Air weapon control commands.

Performance characteristics

'BARS' provides as follows: simultaneous firing of up to four targets in the long-range air combat and one target in the close air combat by 'Air-to-Air' weapons;

Together with OEPrNK it provides the application of 'Air-to-Ground' and Air-to-Air' weapons;

Participating in fighter combat operation control;

Control of flight while applying weapons;

Data interaction with the aircraft avionics and the IFF interrogator;

Estimation of the radar equipment status;

Application of 'Air-to-Air' guided missiles with RDR as leading channel;

Application of 'Air-to-Ground' weapons with RDR as leading channel together with OEPrNK.

Air-to-Air operation modes:
Target detection (velocity search, range search);
Track-while-scan of up to 15 targets and discrete tracking of up to four targets preserving sector surveillance;
Jammer tracking;
Illumination of targets and transmission of radio correction commands for 'Air-to-Air' weapons control;
Assessment of group target characteristics;
Tracking of visually visible targets in close manoeuvrable combat;
Recognition of an air target type upon its spectral characteristics while discrete tracking.

'Air-to-Ground' operation modes:
Real beam mapping;
Mapping in Doppler beam sharpening mode (DBS);
Mapping in SAR mode (synthetic aperture radar);
Ground moving target selection (GMTS);
Tracking and coordinate measurement of up to two ground (surface) targets.

Combined mode:
Tracking of two ground targets preserving sector surveillance for air targets or firing upon one air target in the long-range combat.

'Air-to-Sea' operation modes:
Sea surface surveillance and sea target detection;
Sea moving target selection;
Coordinate measurement of a moving and fixed sea target.

'Air-to-Air':

Detection of a MiG-29 type target in 300 sq. deg. scanning zone as follows:
at head-on courses – up to 140 km;
at trailing courses – up to 60 km.

'Air-to-Ground' mode:

Detection ranges are as follows:
Of a railway bridge: 80-120 km;
Of a group of tanks: 40-50 km;
Of a torpedo boat destroyer: 80-120 km;
Of an aircraft carrier: 250 km.
Maximum resolution is 10-20 m.

Application

Radar control system RLSU 'BARS' is intended for modified multi-target export aircraft versions of Su-30MKI, Su-30MKI(A), Su-30MKM under foreign customer contracts

BARS provides for the following combat modes:
Discrete tracking, preparation and simultaneous homing of 'Air-to-Air' guided missiles RVV-AE, 27R(ER), 27T(ET), 73E while firing upon 1 to 4 targets in the long-range air combat;
'Air-to-Air' guided missiles RVV-AE, 27R(ER), 27T(ET), 73E and built-in guns are applied for firing in close-range air combat modes;
Tracking (of up to two ground or sea targets), preparation and homing on one guided missile X-31A upon a sea target;
Tracking, transmission of preliminary target designation to OEPrNK to fire upon a ground target with guided 'Air-to-Ground' weapons as well as unguided bombs;
During the attack of one ground target RLSU provides for simultaneous detection of air targets or firing upon one target in the long-range air combat under combined mode;
Transmission of data to ACS (automatic control system) and display systems to control the fighter flight under the attack in 'Air-to-Air', Air-to-Sea' and 'Air-to-Ground' modes;

Estimation of equipment and weapon status at all stages of ground preparation and in flight;

Transmission of data to record parameters by the system of objective control SOC;

Operation under active passive jamming conditions and tracking of one jammer with the subsequent attack in FWD and TAIL hemispheres.

In group actions mode the radar provides for the target data acquisition and transmission of target designation (target detection within a group of aircraft) to wingmen; the execution of the attack (combat application) by each wingmen in a group upon four air targets or one ground (sea) target.

Upgrade

Upon the desire of the customer the following changes can be incorporated into RLSU 'BARS':

Antenna diameter and type (PESA – AESA);

Transmission power $P_{aver} = 1...5$ kw;

Applied 'Air-to-Air' and 'Air-to-Ground' weapons of Russian and customers origin are subject to change;

Modes of dangerous moisture target detection are subject to be implemented.

Bars radar system installed in a test aircraft, probably Su-27M. JSC Corporation Irkut

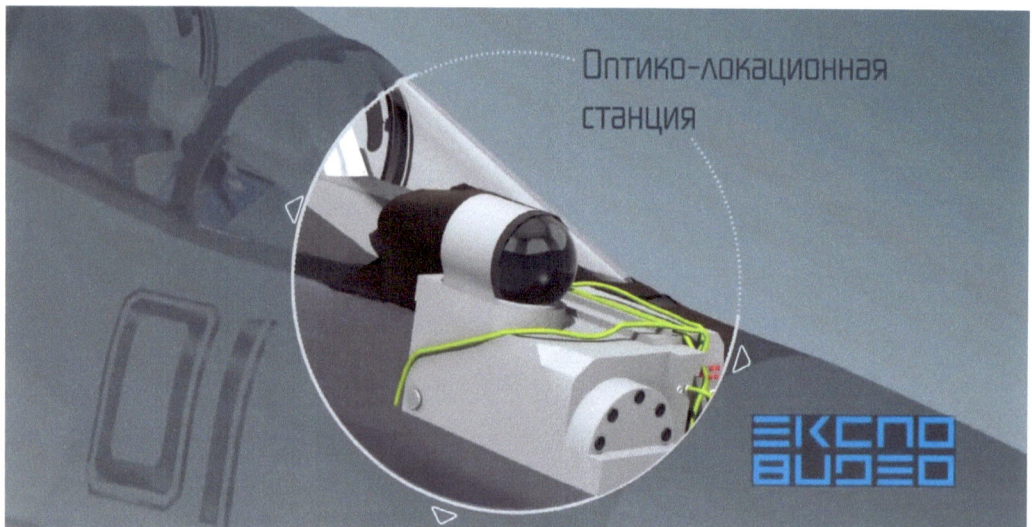

Оптико-локационная станция

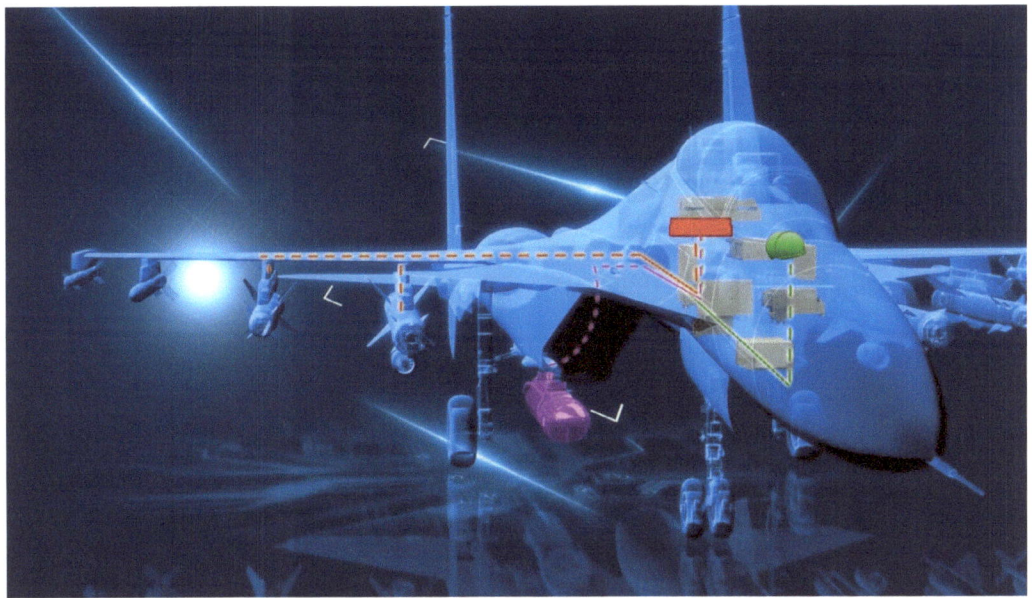

Previous page: The Su-30MKI and derivatives are equipped with an OLS system which allows passive detection, tracking and engagement against air and surface targets. UAC

Above: Integrated with fire control and avionics systems, the OEPrNK-30MKI system transmits targeting information from the aircraft sensors such as the OLS, or external systems such as a navigation and targeting pod, to the aircraft weapons prior to launch. RPKB

Integrated with the radar and other system via the OEPrNK-30MKI, the Su-30MKI family features an integrated electro-optical sighting system and combined navigation system with laser inertial navigation and a satellite navigation receiver that is compatible with the Russian GLONASS and US NAVSTAR clusters, enabling the aircraft to fly precise ingress and egress routes in a target area.

The OLS system itself consists of a number of components of the Optical Electronic Sighting System OEPS-27MK (Article 31E-MK), Optical Location System OLS-27MK (Article 52Sh). Note: some sources state that the OEPS-27MK and OLS-27MK are designated OEPS-30 and OLS-30 respectively, however, this appears to be erroneous as relevant documentation indicates that these systems are designated OEPS-27MK and OLS-27MK respectively.

The OLS provides the Su-30MK family with a passive (radar silent – non-emitting of radar emissions) detection, tracking and engagement capability, reducing the overall vulnerability to enemy direct and indirect detection, tracking and engagement systems and countermeasures. The OLS can also be employed in conjunction with the radar system.

The OLS-27MK (OLS-30) IRST/LR unit, which was developed by the UMAZ (Urals Opto-mechanical plant) is an IR (Infra-Red) and a laser channel and can be used to track ground and airborne targets, determining target position and range.

The system, which weighs less than 180 kg, has a 120° azimuth FOV (Field Of View) and can be elevated +60°/-15°. The system, has a claimed range of around 90 km for a target heading away from the frontal aspect and around 40 km for a target in the head-on aspect.

As stated above, the radar and OLS targeting and surveillance systems are completely integrated with the electronic navigation/attack system, INS (Inertial Navigation System), SATNAV (Satellite Navigation), Laser Gyro and GPS (Global Positioning System) systems through the OEPrNK-30MKI.

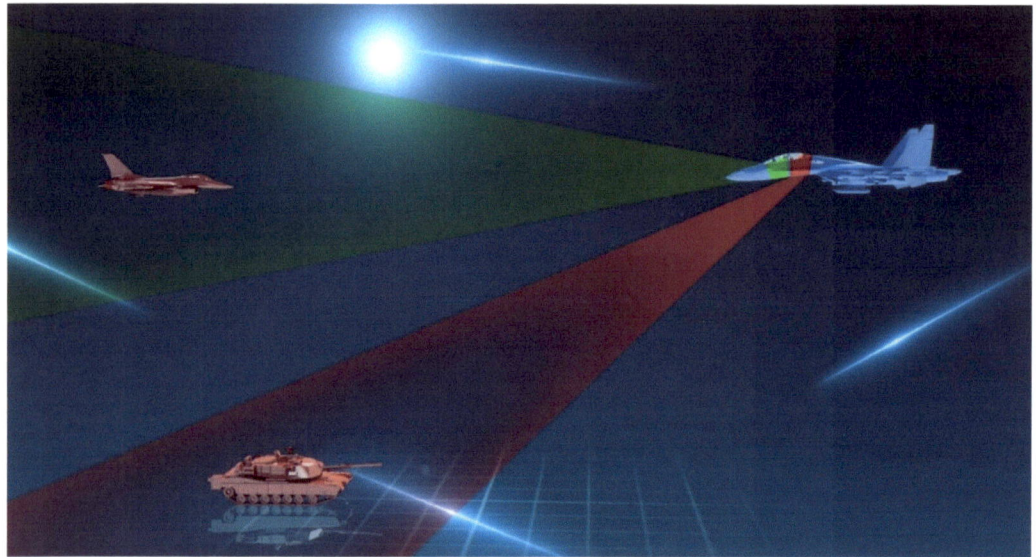

The OEPrNK-30MKI facilitates the ability for the aircraft to simultaneously scan for, detect, track and engage airborne and ground targets. In such scenarios, typically the front cockpit occupant would concentrate on the air to air role whilst the rear cockpit occupant engaged ground targets. RPKB

The avionics suite is sourced from a number of companies in several different countries resulting in the Su-30MKI and the Malaysian Su-30MKM having the most advanced sensor/avionics suites of any Su-27 derivatives, until the advent of the Su-35S, which entered service with the Russian Federation Air Force in 2014. RPKB developed the main Russian components of the avionics suite including the mission computer and was also responsible for overall avionics integration in cooperation with an IAF Project Team based in Moscow.

SAGEM of France provided the GPS navigation system and the MFD-55 and MFD-56 MFDS (Multi-Function Display Screens). France also supplies the Totem INS (Inertial Guidance System) that is integrated with the GPS. EL-OP of Israel is claimed as the supplier for the HUD (Heads-Up-Display), although conflicting documentation states that the heliographic HUD is a VEH 3000 unit sourced in France. The pilot in the front cockpit is equipped with a HMSS (Helmet Mounted Sight System) which is capable of designating targets for the air to air missiles and air to surface weapons.

The Su-30MKI, MKM and MKI(A) are equipped with a SURA HMTDS (Helmet Mounted Target Designation System) while Su-30SM is equipped with the SURA-M, this latter system also equipping the ZS-10 helmet of the Su-35S. On all Su-30 platforms, including the Su-30MK2 family which is equipped with the SURA-K, the target designation system is apparently attached to a ZS-7 flight helmet. Future upgrades could see the Su-30MKI series equipped with the SURA-I HMTDIS (Helmet Mounted Target Designation and Indication System) which is stated by Promoboronexport to have been adopted for the Su-30 series. Longer term more advanced systems are being studied for integration on the Su-30MKI and Su-30MKM, the Thales Topsight system being specifically mentioned, although this may be subject to change.

The HMTDS, together with the 6231R-9-2 IFF interrogator, completes the weapons control system. The SURA and SURA-M, can, according to manufacturer documentation, scan the airspace $\pm$ 70° in azimuth and -35° to +65° in elevation with a designation accuracy (RMS error) of < 3 mrad. The entire system weighs 10 kg (SURA) and 6 kg (SURA-M), the helmet mounted element weighting 0.39 kg.

In simplified terms the HMTDS, which receives signal inputs from the various on-board systems, displays flight and targeting information on a visor on the pilot flight helmet. This data, which is displayed in symbolic and alphanumeric form, with various data types and volumes specified by individual operators, is projected on a field of view of 6°x4°.

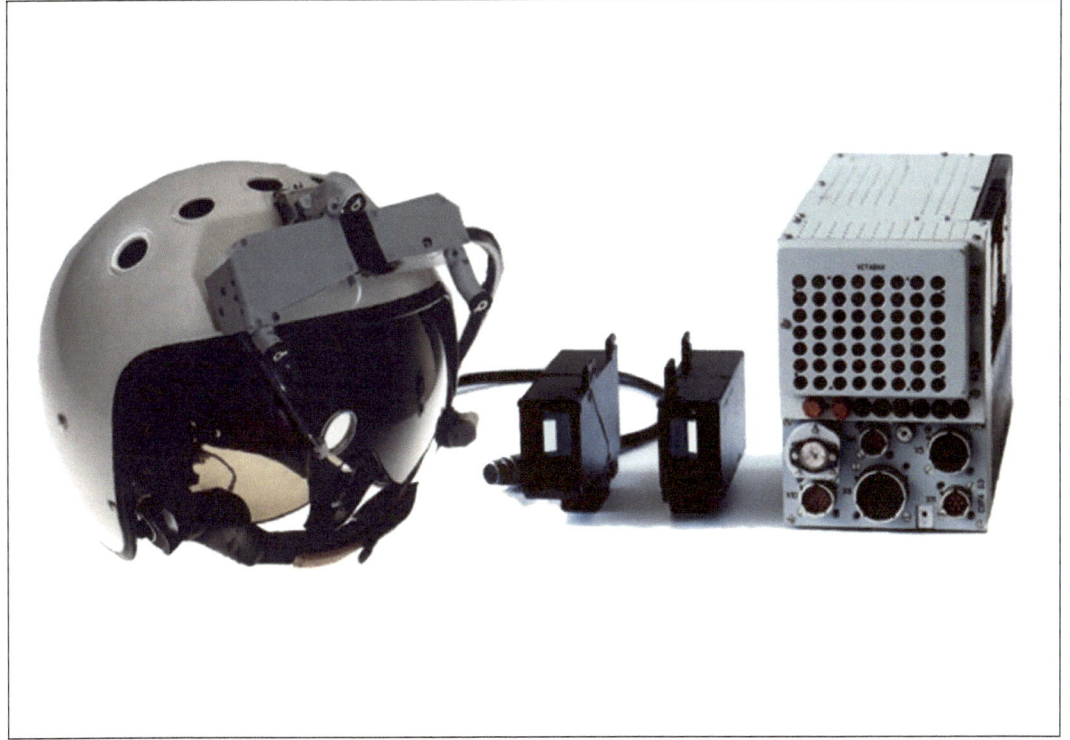

The SURA-I (above) is visually representative of the SURA and SURA-K HMTDS.

The display system in the Su-30MKI consists of three MFD-55 colour multi-function display screens in each cockpit, and a single MFD-56 colour display in the rear cockpit and a wide-angle HUD atop the dashboard of the front cockpit. RPKB

The Su-30MKI communications suite consists of VHF (Very High Frequency) and HF (High Frequency) radio and a digitally secure telecommunications system. The flight data recorder can be used in a secondary function to record data relating to the tactical situation.

Threats are detected by the Tarang MK II RWR (Radar Warning Receiver). This system is integrated with chaff and flare dispensers and the on-board active radar jamming system. The self-defence suite also features UV (Ultra Violet) irradiation of attacking missiles.

Production standard Su-30MKI aircraft are equipped with the K-36D-3.5 zero-zero ejection seats in both cockpits as installed in the Su-30MKK/MK2 family. The manufacturer description reads, "The crewmember protection against the dynamic pressure G-loads at ejection is provided with the protection gear, windblast shield, forced restraint in the seat, seat stabilization as well as the selection of one of three operation modes for the emergency source depending on the suited pilot mass. At the aircraft speed exceeding 850 km/h, the MRM steady-state mode is adjusted by the automatics depending on the acceleration."

"After automatic separation of the pilot from the seat, the recovery parachute canopy is inflated providing the pilot's safe descent. A portable survival kit, which is separated from the seat together with the pilot, supports his/her vital functions after landing or water landing, makes the pilot search easier, and the… -1 life raft supports the pilot floatation on the surface of the water."

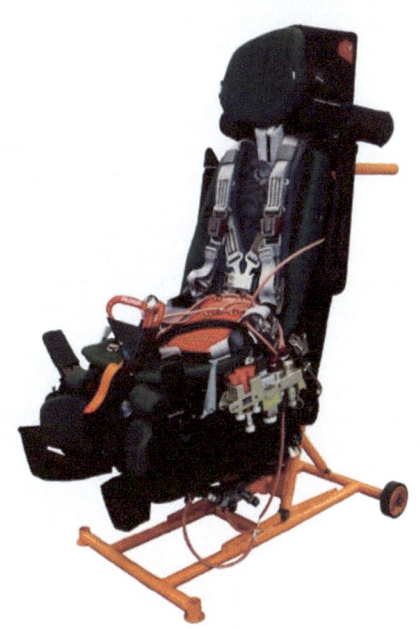

Top: The two-crew members are seated in the stepped tandem cockpit layout original introduced on the Su-27UB, although equipment fit is different. UAC **Above: All variants of the Su-30MKI family are equipped with Zvezda K-36D-3.5 zero zero ejection seats. The seats equipping the domestic Su-30SM variant are modified compared to the standard export model.** NPP Zvezda

"The K-36D-3.5 ejection seat realizes the crew member emergency escape within the range of equivalent airspeed (VE) from 0 to 1300 km/h, at Mach number up to 2.5 and aircraft flight altitude from 0 to 20000 m, including takeoff, landing run and H=0, V=0 mode. The seat is used with the KKO-15 set of protective gear and oxygen equipment." The weight of the seat and survival kit is around 103 kg.

The K-36D-3.5 seat, development of which was completed in 2001, are apparently inclined at an angle of 30°. As with the Su-27UB, the seat in the rear cockpit is raised compared to the front seat, improving the forward view of the rear seat occupant.

The pilot life-support system includes the NPP Zvezda KC-129, specified for the Su-30MKM and Su-30MKI(A), but probably also installed in the Su-30SM, which supplies both crew with oxygen supply for operations up to 20 km, in excess of 2000 m higher than the Su-30MKI series normal operating ceiling. The system is referred to as a "bottle-free oxygen system" by the manufacturer as the oxygen is generated from compressed air taken from the gas turbine compressor. This means there is no requirement for on-board oxygen cylinders, reducing the pre-flight preparation requirements with the added benefit that mission duration is not limited due to oxygen cylinder supply.

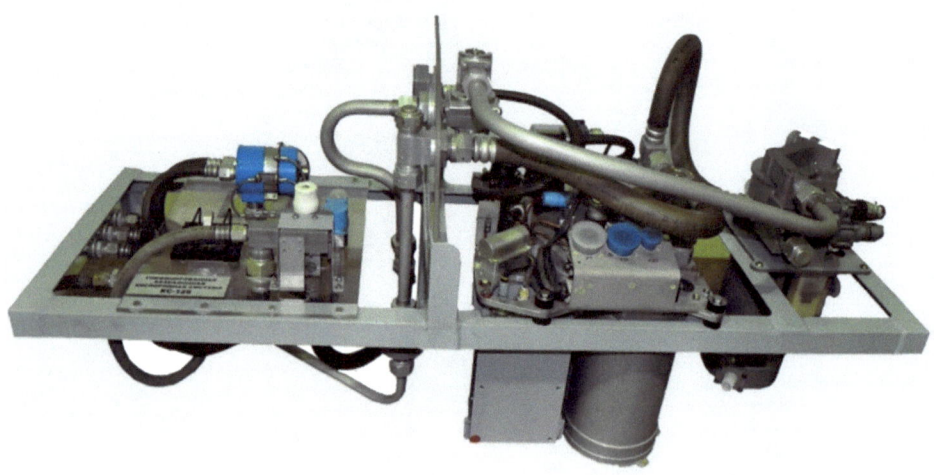

The pilot life-support system includes the NPP Zvezda KC-129 in the Su-30MKM and Su-30MKI(A). A variation of this system is probably installed on the Domestic Su-30SM procured for the Russian Federation Air Force and Russian Naval Aviation.
NPP Zvezda

The Su-30MKI series can carry a maximum load of 8000 kg on twelve external stations, some of which can accommodate multiple ejector racks. As with other members of the Su-30MK family, the Su-30MKI and derivatives can employ a wide diversity of guided and unguided air to air and air to surface weapons which are detailed in chapter 6.

There was no requirement to build a prototype for the Su-30MKM for Malaysia or the Su-30MKI(A) for Algeria, although a number of the JSC Corporation Irkut fleet of pre-production Su-30MKI's were utilised, with modifications, to test elements of the respective designs. JSC Corporation Irkut

As with other members of the Su-30 family, design of the Su-30MKM ordered by Malaysia for the RMAF (Royal Malaysian Air Force) was conducted by Sukhoi JSC, the aircraft being built by Irkut Corporation. The contract schedule called for delivery of six aircraft in June 2006, followed by six more aircraft by the end of that year, with the final batch of six aircraft to be delivered in 2007, although deliveries ran outside this schedule, the last of the eighteen aircraft ordered being delivered in 2009.

The Su-30MKM was developed from the Su-30MKI built for India, both variants having much in common, such as the canard tri-plane layout and thrust-vector control for the engine nozzles. Whilst having a common airframe, powerplant, digital flight control and fire control systems – Bars radar and OLS (these systems being more or less identical to those systems found in the Su-30MKI) – with the Su-30MKI, the Su-30MKM differed from the former in some areas of equipment fit.

The Su-30MKM avionics system is based, to a large extent, on that found in the Su-30MKI. However, there are some differences as Malaysia wished to replace items installed in the Su-30MKI that were sourced from Israel. This decision, which has been attributed to being a political protest against Israel's oppression of the Palestinian peoples, may simply be a decision to source the most advanced systems available for the Su-30MKM. In December 2003, Thales of France signed a contract valued at €150 million Euros covering supply and integration of various avionics equipment including navigation, identification and optronics systems for the Su-30MKM. The integration of such systems was to be conducted by Thales in Russia under leadership of the prime contractor, JSC Sukhoi, with a RMAF project team based in Moscow overseeing the work.

Non-Russian sourced equipment includes the Thales wide-angle HUD, integrated radio and electro-optic systems, FLIR – Thales Damocles NAVFLIR (Navigation Forward Looking Infrared) pod which allows targets to be designated and attacked day and night and in adverse weather conditions. In the Su-30MKI the primary digital computer is Russian sourced whilst the secondary digital computer is sourced from India. In the Su-30MKM both primary and secondary digital computers are Russian designed and built. Common to both the MKI and MKM are the six 5 x 5 in MFD-55 displays MFDS – three in each cockpit. The rear cockpit is also furnished with a single 6 x 6 in MFD-66 MFDS,

Antenna protrusions for the French sourced IFF are located forward of the cockpit windscreen on top of the aircraft nose section.

The Saab Group LWS-310 laser illumination warning system (above) is installed on the fleet of eighteen Su-30MKM multirole fighter aircraft delivered to the Royal Malaysian Air Force; this being only one element of an integrated self-defence suite that includes the Saab Group MAW-300 Passive UV (Ultra Violet) based sensors illustrated on page 63. Saab Group

The LWS-310 laser illumination warning and MAW-300 missile approach warning elements of the self-defence suite were sourced from Avitronics (now part of the Saab Group) in South Africa. The LWS-310 consists of 4 sensors and a processor card included in the EWC (Electronic Warfare Controller). The manufacturer states that the system "features high sensitivity. Excellent Threat Coverage and exceptional Probability of Intercept, POI, for single as well as multi-pulse emissions." The system is not only capable of classifying laser emissions, but, as pointed out by the manufacturer, can also identify such emissions through a "User Programmable Threat Library".

The following information is provided by the manufacturer: "The system features - wavelength coverage of 0.5-1.7 µm; provides threat classification and direction finding indication of laser range finders, designators, lasers used for missile guidance and dazzler lasers; identify specific lasers if threat library information is available; high sensitivity to detect missile guidance lasers, high probability of intercept; low false alarm rate; spatial coverage 360° AZ with four sensors including good sensor overlap; direction finding to allow appropriate manoeuvring to break operators line of sight and counter threats; provision for up to (6) sensors for improved large platform coverage."

The Su-30MKM has four LWS-310 sensors, two covering the front hemisphere being located on the underside of the nose section while an additional two sensors, covering the rear hemisphere, are located on the engine intake outer walls; one on each intake.

The MAW-300, which is described by the manufacturer as a "unique optical design, incorporating filter technology, with purpose-built image intensifier tubes and photon-counting focal-plane array processors", which, continues Saab Group, "ensures high sensitivity equating to long detection range." Each of the systems individual sensors has its own dedicated signal processor having recourse to a "distributed, hierarchical data-processing architecture to ensure optimal utilization of information in real-time."

Each of the individual sensors is capable of detecting and processing multiple targets with the spatial and temporal feature information being transferred to the processor card located in the EWC where it is combined with real-time data from the INS in order to compensate for the linear movement, altitude and attitude.

Manufacturer information shows that the MAW-300 features – "Passive Ultra Violet (UV) based sensors, which operates in the solar blind UV spectrum; Neutral net classifiers using both temporal and accurate spatial information as well as compensation of on platform movement, ensures low false alarm rates; Reaction time optimized by keeping missile time to impact constant, irrespective of range to ensure enhanced flare countermeasures effectiveness; Inhibits warning against diverging missiles; Direction accuracy suitable for cueing DIRCM and dispensing of countermeasures decoys in correct direction; Spatial coverage of 110° conical per sensor limits unprotected 'hole' below platform and allows good sensor overlap; Spatial coverage 360° AZ with 4 sensors. Full spherical coverage can be achieved with six sensors. Provision to add up to eight sensors to ensure hemispherical or full spherical coverage; Multi-threat capability allows tracking of multiple targets simultaneously; Near 100% probability of warning; In production for numerous platforms; Field tested and qualified various missiles including live missile firings under in-flight dynamic conditions; compact, lightweight, low power, no cooling, skin mounted sensors."

The MAW-300 sensors are located on the nose section underside, a three sensor cluster, and another UV sensor group is located on the aircraft spine roughly halfway between the spine mounted airbrake and bulged engine housing. The two UV sensor groups provide spherical coverage against threats.

Russian designed elements of the self-defence suite include the RWR and ECM systems, much of the latter can be housed in wingtip mounted pods. The domestic Su-30SM is certainly equipped with wingtip mounted electronic warfare sensor pods; apparently the L175M Khibiny-M self-defence pods as specified for the Su-35S or a variation of this equipment, which, as yet, is not cleared for export.

The expendable elements of the self-defence suite consist of the Russian designed passive infrared/chaff dispensers located in the aircraft tail section. This system contains a battery of 98 chaff/flare cartridges.

4

SU-30MKI/MKM/MKI(A) PRODUCTION AND SERVICE

The phased production of the Su-30MK (MKI) for the IAF (Indian Air Force) called for increasingly more capable specifications with enhancements to the avionics and weapon systems as well as integration of additional weapons. Only the final batch of 22 aircraft from the original 32 aircraft ordered in late 1996 were to be delivered to the full Su-30MKI standard. The first Su-30's featuring thrust-vector control for the engine nozzles were initially to be delivered to India in 1999. However, this date was put back due to program slips, on top of which the program was affected by technical troubles, mainly concerning western avionics to be fitted to the aircraft which contributed in no small order to the slippage in delivery schedules. Political scandal also had a detrimental effect on the program, and in late 1999 an enquiry was ordered into the acquisition process.

Production of the Su-30MKI commenced at IAPA in 2000, the first pre-production aircraft, coded Blue 05, conducting its maiden flight with Vyacheslav Averyanov at the controls on 26 November that year, Blue 04 was shown at Aero India in Bangalore in early February 2001. The fourth pre-production Su-30MKI was handed over to Sukhoi on 11 August 2001, joining the three other pre-production aircraft in a flight test program, together with the surviving prototype, Blue 06. The pre-production Su-30MKI's were equipped with operational fire control system/avionics suites.

The Su-30MKI contract was divided into three phases and IAPA began deliveries of the first batch in late June 2002, and completed delivery of the batch of ten aircraft by September that year. These aircraft, which were delivered to Lohegaon Air Base as air-freight on-board An-124 Ruslan transport aircraft, formally entered service with No.20 squadron IAF at Pune on 27 September 2002. A second batch of 12 aircraft and a final batch of ten aircraft were delivered by the end of 2003, and by 2004 the 18 Su-30K and 32 Su-30MKI's ordered in 1996 were serving with two squadrons of the IAF.

The IAF has ordered 272 Su-30MKI's in several separate contracts since 1996. UAC

The first ten Su-30MKI's were known as Stage I or Phase 1, which was optimised for the air to air role. The Phase 2 Su-30MKI' added a number of additional capabilities including the integration of the Kh-31A air to surface missile and introduced increased air to air functionality by incorporating the capability to engage up to four targets simultaneously. As well as enhancements to the radar the second phase added a digital map and had provision for adding the Kh-59M TV (Television) guided air to ground missile.

The full standard Su-30MKI specification was incorporated into the Phase 3 production aircraft. Additional capabilities included the ability to engage four targets simultaneously in the frontal and rear hemispheres. Enhancements to the available radar modes allowed the engagement of surface targets, while continuing to search for airborne targets in the air to air modes while engaging an airborne target. The radar standard fitted in the phase three Su-30MKI also featured the full spectrum of navigation and combat modes and was capable of designating targets for weapons launch while the aircraft was conducting highly agile manoeuvres in the so called 'super-manoeuvrability' mode. The last of the third phase deliveries, from the contract signed in November 1996, serial SB041, was delivered in late 2003.

On 28 December 2000, India signed a contract for license production of up to 140 Su-30 MKI's at HAL (Hindustan Aeronautics Limited) Nasik facility. This production program was scheduled to continue through to 2017, with India producing engines, aircraft systems and avionics. Information emanating from HAL indicates that there are some 157 sub-contractors on the Su-30MKI program in India.

HAL builds the canards, stabilizers and under-boom ventral fins under a contract agreement signed between Irkut Corporation and HAL in 2003. Fuel systems, pneumatic and hydraulic systems are manufactured in Lucknow. Electronics systems, including the radar, were to be manufactured at Hyderabad. Some avionics systems were to be manufactured in Koro. The computers apparently incorporate a pair of digital processors developed by India's DRDO (Defence Research & Development Organisation) subsidiary, DARE (Defence Avionics Research Establishment); DARE also developed the Tarang RWR and communications systems and IFF systems were developed by HAL at Hyderabad. Display screens for the cockpit and GPS systems are manufactured in Korwa. Aircraft kits are assembled at HAL Nasik and AL-31FP engines are built from kits supplied to HAL's Korput Plant by JSC UMPO.

By late 2004, HAL was conducting flight tests with the first two license built Su-30MKI's at its Nasik facility. The first licence produced aircraft, assembled from kits supplied by Russia, had conducted its maiden flight on 1 October 2004; the first two licence built Su-30MKI's being formally accepted by the IAF on 28 November that year.

While these aircraft were built from kits supplied from Russia, as the program progressed Indian contribution to supply would increase, including supply of hydraulic and pneumatic systems noted above.

Page 68-69: On 13 July 2008, IAF Su-30MKI's transited through Lajes Field in the Azores Islands en-route to the USA to participate in a Red Flag exercise. USAF

A further contract for the supply of an additional 40 Su-30MKI's direct from Russia was signed in February 2007. The requirement for the additional Su-30MKI's was in response to delays in India's program to purchase around 126 combat aircraft to replace older aircraft in service, many of which would have to be retired before the planned replacements were available. The desire to maintain, or at least slow the decline in squadron levels, was probably hardened by Pakistan's continued purchase of military hardware from the United States, with a US administration decision to sell Pakistan an additional 36 F-16 multi-role fighter aircraft. Around this time, India's Cabinet Committee on Security revealed plans to speed up delivery of the license produced Su-30MKI's, 34 of which had been produced by India under licence by late summer 2008, according to information furnished by Sukhoi Design Bureau.

From the earliest deliveries there was speculation, often presented as fact, that the first two batches of Su-30MKI's would be upgraded to the standard specified for the batch three deliveries. However, it was not until January 2006 that representatives from HAL, DRDO and their Russian counterparts formally met to thrash out the particulars of such an upgrade, which commenced in 2007. Suggestions that the 18 Su-30K's, purchased as interim equipment pending Su-30MKI deliveries, should be upgraded to Su-30MKI standard were dismissed as being economically unsound. It was therefore determined that these aircraft would be returned to Russia, India purchasing 18 additional Su-30MKI's direct from Russia as replacements, a contract for such being signed in April 2007, by which time the IAF operated something in the order of 50 Su-30MKI's from Pune, Bareily and Halwara. The Su-30K's were subsequently purchased by Angola (12) and Iraq (6) with a delivery schedule between 2015 and 2017, following refurbishment at the 558th Aviation Repair Plant in

Belarus.

Page 70-71: An Indian Air Force Su-30MKI detachment arrives at Nellis AFB, Nevada, USA, on 6 August 2008, to participate in a Red Flag exercise. USAF

Page 72-73: Ground operations of the Indian Su-30MKI detachment at Nellis AFB, Nevada, USA, on 13 and 19 August 2008. USAF

Page 74-76: IAF Su-30MKI during training sorties with RAF Eurofighter Typhoon and Tornado F.3 fighter/interceptors; the latter type being retired in 2011. RAF

By early 2009. Irkut had delivered 100 Su-30 aircraft or component packages to India, with the latter being used to produce aircraft in India under licence. As deliveries continued apace the IAF ordered a further 42 Su-30MKI's on 24 December 2012; these aircraft to be assembled from kits supplied by Russia under a contract valued at around US $1.6 Billion. The IAF received its 200th (the 150th licence produced) Su-30MKI on 9 January 2015. When deliveries from all contracts are complete the IAF will have taken delivery of 272 Su-30MKI's.

IAF Su-30MKI's on the ramp at Nellis AFB, Nevada, with USAF F-15 Eagle air superiority fighters in the background. Over the course of several exercises the IAF Su-30MKI pilots were left with a pleasing assessment of their mounts ability to defeat aircraft in the class of the F-15. JSC Corporation Irkut

As the Su-30MKI was establishing itself in IAF service, the Su-30K's participated in USAF exercises, during the course of which it was deemed that the Su-30K had got the better of USAF F-15C Eagle fighters during a series of mock-engagements. The apparent superiority of the Su-30MKI over the F-15 appeared to be confirmed during exercise Cope India in November 2005. Further exercises, which pitted the Su-30MKI against its western counterparts, including USAF F-15's, and RAF Eurofighter Typhoons, left a marked impression on potential adversaries.

Around the mid-2000's, several reports quoted an unreleased USAF document stating that F-15 fighters had performed poorly against Su-30MKIs in the series of exercises; this being added to by IAF pilot reports singing a similar tune. The USAF F-15 fighters referred to, based at Elmendorf AFB, Alaska, were the most advanced in USAF service, equipped with APG-63(V)2 radar fitted with an AESA (Active Electronically Scanned Array) affording far superior performance to the mechanically scanned antenna equipping the vast majority of the USAF F-15A/B/C/D fleet.

Page 78-80: Indian Air Force Su-30MKI's during a training operation. JSC Corporation Irkut

Two of a trio of Indian Air Force Su-30MKI's perform a lateral break, port and starboard, as the third continues on its linear trajectory. JSC Corporation Irkut

During the series of air defence exercises the Indian Su-30's and the USAF F-15's were apparently detecting each other at roughly the same distances. However, the Indians, in their Su-30's (Su-30K equipped with N001 radar and Su-30MKI equipped with N011 Bars radar), were able to get off the first simulated missile shots with the R-27 AA-10 'Alamo' air to air missiles, enabling the Su-30 to win the long range engagements against the F-15's and their simulated Raytheon AIM-120 AMRAAM (Advanced Medium Range Air to Air Missile) active radar guided air to air missiles.

During the Red Flag exercise held in the US in August 2008, the IAF Su-30MKI crews were restricted in the use of radar in order to reduce the gains of the electronic intelligence net cast by the USAF to garner information on the capability of the Bars radar system. Despite these restrictions the Su-30MKI apparently demonstrated measures of superiority in both medium range and close-range air to air engagements with USAF F-15C fighters. In the medium range engagements the IAF pilots were able to detect, lock-on and launch simulated missiles before the F-15C.

While the capabilities of the Su-30MKI was being demonstrated against foreign air forces in a number of exercise scenarios, the IAF fleet continued to establish itself in service with the equipment of No.30 Squadron, 'Charging Rhinos'. With deliveries of licence produced aircraft additional squadrons would equip with the Su-30MKI, which would eventually constitute the backbone of the IAF defensive and offensive air power capabilities in the second decade of the 21st century.

The deliveries of progressively more capable Su-30MKI's dramatically increased the defensive and offensive capabilities of the IAF. These capabilities would be further increased with the delivery of the three A-50I AWACS (Airborne Warning and Control System) platforms in the first half of the 2010's. The A-50I, combined with the Su-30MKI's long range, would revolutionise the IAF's airspace defence and power projection capabilities.

The Royal Malaysian Air Force acquired a fleet of eighteen Su-30MKM which differed from the Indian Su-30MKI only in certain items of the avionics suite. JSC Corporation Irkut

The road to Malaysia's Su-30 purchase began with the issuing of an MRCA (Multi-Role Combat Aircraft) requirement in the late 1990's. In January 2001, Malaysian news reported that the country was finalising a deal for a Su-30 purchase under the designation Su-30MKM (Modernised Commercial Malaysian). Malaysia was seeking the Su-30MKM multi-role fighters to replace seven obsolete Northrop (now Northrop Grumman) F-5E lightweight fighters. The Su-30's would supplement the RMAF (Royal Malaysian Air Force) MiG-29N fighters in the air to air role and the Boeing F/A-18D Hornet strike fighters in the air to air and air to surface roles.

On 5 August 2003, during a visit to the country by the Russian Federation President, Malaysia ordered eighteen Su-30MKM multirole fighters under a US $900 million contract, the aircraft to be built at Irkut with the last of these being delivered direct from Russia in August 2009; the design having been selected after a stringent analysis of the Su-30MKI derivative and the Boeing F/A-18E/F Super Hornet.

Two pre-production Su-30MKI's, side codes 04 and 05, were apparently fitted out to flight test equipment configurations for the Su-30MKM and the Su-30MKI(A) for Algeria, the first flight in MKM configuration taking place at Zhukovsky, on 23 May 2006, crewed by test pilots Sergey Kostin and Vyacheslav Averyanov. The second of the pre-production aircraft flew in Su-30MKM configuration on 9 June 2006. Flight testing, which was conducted mainly at Zhukovsky and the Russian Federation Defence Ministry (GLIT) State Flight Test Centre, located in Akhtubinsk, was completed in the first third of 2007, by which time serial production of the Su-30MKM had commenced at the Irkutsk production plant.

The first two serial production Su-30MKM's were officially handed over to the RMAF in an acceptance ceremony at Irkutsk on 24 May 2007. On the 18th of the following month these two aircraft were delivered as air freight by An-124 Ruslan heavy-lift transport aircraft to Gong Kedak air base, Kelantan Province, on the eastern coast of the Malay Peninsula. A further two Su-30MKM's were delivered on 10 August 2007.

Delivery of the first handful of Su-30MKM's allowed conversion training to start in earnest, aided by a cadre of three Sukhoi test pilots, Yevgeny Frolov, Sergey Bogdan and Sergey Kostin. Training of Malaysian crews was conducted in time to allow a trio of Malaysian piloted Su-30MKM's to be flown in the air segment of the 50th anniversary of Malaysia's independence from the United Kingdom, on 31 August 2007.

Two Su-30MKM's conducted demonstration flights at the 8th International Aviation and Maritime Defence Show – LIMA-2007 in December 2007, flown by the first pilots from the RMAF 11 Squadron, based at Gong Kedak, to qualify on the aircraft. The two Su-30MKM' flew a spirited display over Langkawi.

The last four aircraft from the last batch of six of the eighteen aircraft ordered were delivered to Malaysia by An-124 transport aircraft by the end of November 2009.

Algeria operates a force of 44 Su-30MKI(A) multirole fighters. The Su-30MKI(A) is based on the Indian Su-30MKI, with thrust-vectoring and canard triplane configuration, but features some differences in equipment fit. A contract for the purchase of 28 Su-30's for Algeria, signed between that nation and Russia's Rosoboronexport in 2006, called for the delivery of the 28 aircraft between 2007 and 2009. The first two Su-30MKI(A) were delivered from the Irkutsk plant to Sukhoi Design Bureau in summer 2007, these being incorporated into a trials program conducted in cooperation with the GLIT test centre at Akhtubinsk

Manufacture of a further three Su-30MKI(A) was completed in September 2007, these aircraft going to the Gromov LII facility at Zhukovsky to be used in conversion training of a cadre of Algerian Air Force pilots. Once the training program was complete the aircraft and pilots would be transferred to Algeria; the initial five aircraft being joined by one more Su-30MKI(A) around December 2007/January 2008, facilitating for the delivery to the Algerian Air Force of a batch of six aircraft by early 2008. The balance of 22 aircraft from the initial contract being delivered to Algeria during 2008 and 2009.

In March 2010, Algeria ordered a further 16 Su-30MKI(A), in effect converting the options on the aircraft from the 2006 contract; these aircraft replacing Algeria's previous planned purchase of MiG-29SMT/UBT multirole fighter aircraft. Algeria also began receiving Yak-130 advanced trainer aircraft from 2010, facilitating advanced pilot training for pilots going on to fly the Su-30MKI(A).

Algeria operates a fleet of 44 Su-30MKI(A) multirole fighters, eleven of which can be observed in this satellite image. Algeria also operates a small fleet of Yak-130 advanced jet trainers which are used to train pilots before they transition to the Su-30MKI(A).

5

SU-30SM(CM) – RUSSIAN DOMESTIC SUPER-MANOEUVRABLE FIGHTER

In the second half of 2011, it was becoming evident that the Russian Federation Air Force and naval air arm would order a number of Su-30SM (Su-30CM in Russian language documentation), a variant of the Su-30MKI series optimised for the Russian Federation Air Force and naval air arm, a batch of 28 aircraft with 12 options then being referred to. Although an order for such was not expected until sometime the following year, Irkut Corporation, in 2011, commenced manufacture of two aircraft facilitating early testing once a production order was placed.

The Su-30SM replaces much of the foreign sourced equipment installed in the export variants with Russian sourced equipment and adds the Khibiny-U EW system. The Bars-R radar element of the fire control system is generally the same unit as installed in export variants, but does incorporate a number of additional operating modes compared to the baseline system. Although no information has been released, it is inferred that the number of airborne targets that can be tracked and simultaneously engaged remains at 15 and 4 respectively, detection range being in the order of 150 km. The pilots' forward view of the outside world is conducted through a wide-angle HUD (Heads up Display) collimator, apparently a variation of the IKSH-1M installed on the Su-35S, although the system installed on the Su-30SM appears visually distinct from the latter while the SURA-M HMTDS replaces the SURA system. The communications systems are optimised for Russian service, as is the undisclosed IFF (Identification Friend or Foe) interrogator which would be in advance of the 6231-R installed on the Su-30MK2. The BINS-SP2 strapdown inertial navigation system which enables the host aircraft to conduct accurate navigation even in the absence of GPS (Global Positioning System) and offshore ground based navigation data. The Zvezda K-36D zero zero ejection seat has been modified to meet domestic requirements along with some other on-board "support systems", as stated by JSC Corporation Irkut. Elements of the self-defence suite that were foreign sourced in the Su-30MKI and Su-30MKM are Russian sourced in the Su-30SM; these including laser warning sensors and ultraviolet irradiation of attacking missiles.

No performance specifications have been released for the Su-30SM, but these, it can be inferred, will be generally the same as those of the Su-30MKI, with a few possible minor differences, thrust output of the AL-31FP engines being generally the same as the export standard engine.

Frontal and rear on aspect views of a Su-30SM. JSC Corporation Irkut

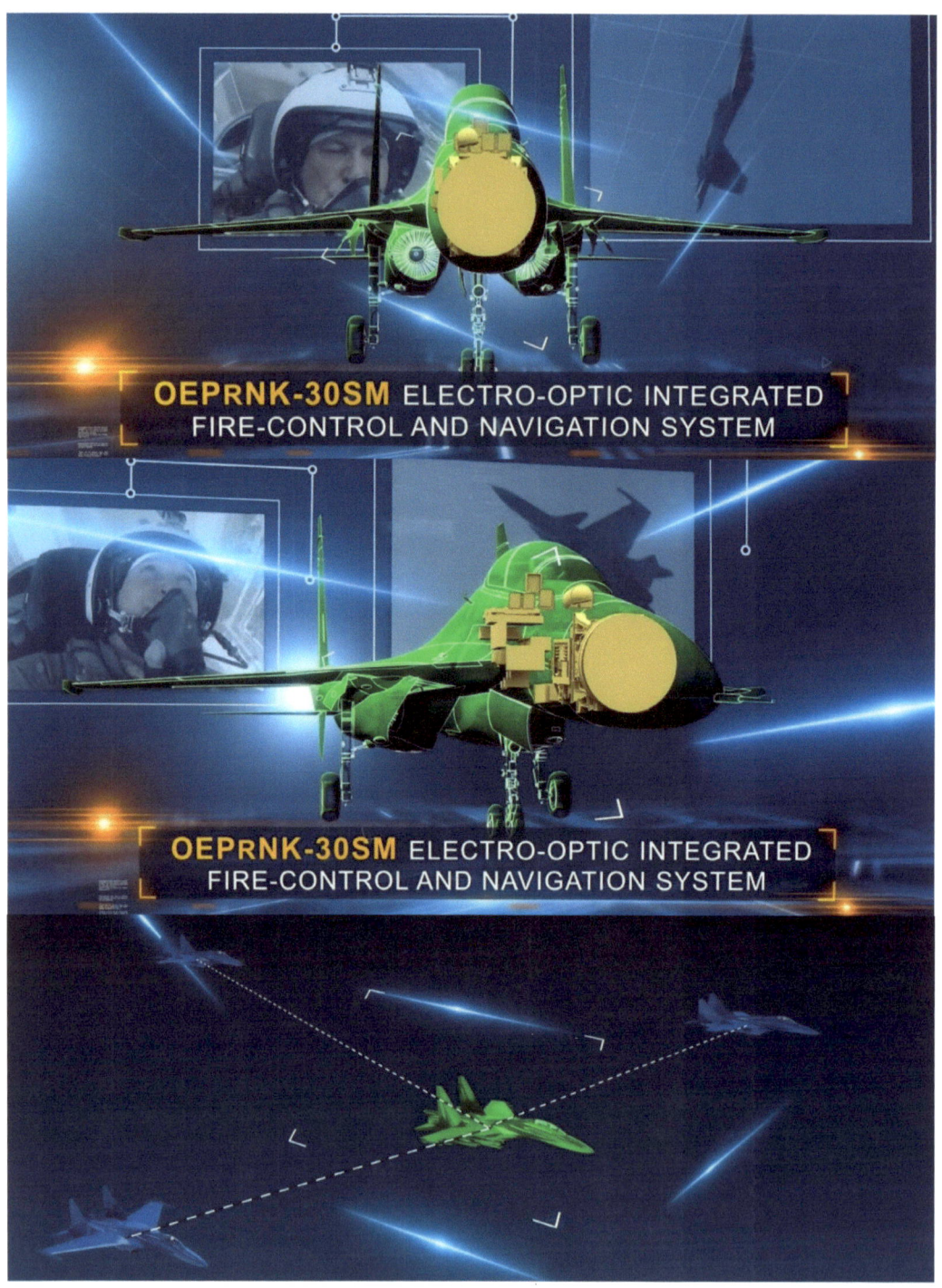

Previous page: Ensemble of computer generated graphics showing side and semi-frontal views of the Su-30SM along with a ghosted view in the centre. This page: Computer generated graphics showing the layout of the OEPrNK-30SM electro-optic integrated fire control and navigation system. The lower graphic illustrates the aircraft relaying tactical data by datalink to other tactical fighter aircraft, in this case Su-27 air superiority fighters. RPKB

Page 89-90: **Su-30SM super-manoeuvrable multirole fighters and Yak-130 advanced jet trainer aircraft during assembly at the Irkutsk Aviation Plant**. JSC Corporation Irkut

Russian Defence Ministry documentation would suggest that the Su-30SM is being viewed as the main Russian Federation Su-27 replacement rather than the Su-35S or the fifth generation T-50, the latter aircraft in particular likely to be procured only in small numbers and only 48 of the former having been procured as of January 2016.

The first contract for delivery of Su-30SM's to the Russian Federation Air Force was signed between the Russian Defence Ministry and JSC Corporation Irkut in March 2012; Irkut announcing on the 22nd of that month that a contract had been signed by Russian Federation Defence Minister Anatoly Serdukov and JSC Corporation Irkut President Alexei Fyodorov for the production of 30 Su-30SM multirole super manoeuvrable fighters for the Russian Federation Air Force. The first two aircraft were to be ready for flight testing later in 2012, with deliveries to the customer scheduled to commence in 2013 and continue through to 2015.

The Su-30SM is a domesticated derivative of the export Su-30MKI. Sukhoi

A further batch of 30 Su-30SM were ordered for the Russian Federation Air Force on 19 December 2012, by which time flight testing of the first aircraft was underway following its maiden flight on 21 September that year at the Irkutsk Aviation Production facility. Crew for the two hour maiden flight was Sukhoi Design Bureau Test Pilot 1st Class Commander Sergey Kostin and navigator Malovchko Pavel of the Russian Federation Air Force; the aircraft, coded 01, still in yellow primer at the time. The second Su-30SM, Su-30SM-02, conducted its maiden flight on 25 September 2012, four days after Su-30SM-01; the crew for the 1 hour 40 minute flight being the same as for Su-30SM-01 on the 21st of the month.

Previous page and above: The first production Su-30SM, Black 01, in a hangar at the Irkutsk Aviation Production facility. This aircraft was the first Su-30SM to fly when it conducted its maiden flight on 21 September 2012. JSC Corporation Irkut

JSC Corporation Irkut handed over the first two Su-30SM to the Russian Federation Air Force in a signing of acceptance ceremony at the Irkutsk plant on 22 November 2012. The introduction of new advanced fighter aircraft was conducted in coordination with the introduction of the Yak-130 advanced trainer aircraft, nine of which had been delivered to the Borisoglebsk training centre by the time of the delivery of the first two Su-30SM's.

After delivery to the Russian Federation Air Force, Su-30SM-01 and 02 were incorporated into the state trials program, operating mainly from the V.P. Chkalov State Flight Test centre at Akhtubinsk. They were joined by Su-30SM-54 in spring 2013, this latter aircraft being noted at Akhtubinsk on 6 May 2013. Towards the end of June 2013, the State Flight Test Centre signed off on what it termed the preliminary conclusion of 'Special Joint Flight Tests'.

In mid-August 2013, the Russian Federation Air Force Commander in Chief, Lt. General Victor Bondarev, stated that the Su-30SM would be fielded at Domna air base in Chita, Eastern Military District, in the Trans Baikal Territory. Prior to this the Lipetsk Aviatsentr accepted (at Irkutsk) its first pair of Su-30SM, 55 and 56, on 13 September 2013, allowing Russian Federation Air Force operational testing to determine operational procedures and tactics for the new multirole fighters. The aircraft arrived at Lipetsk on 14 September, being joined a few weeks later by Su-30SM-57.

The second Su-30SM, Black 02, conducted its maiden flight on 24 September 2012.
JSC Corporation Irkut

Page 95-98: Su-30SM Black 55 cavorts for the camera during a demonstration sortie.
JSC Corporation Irkut

Prior to their delivery to Lipetsk, Su-30SM's, code 55 and 56, were displayed at the MAKS show at Zhukovsky in August 2013. The aircraft were displayed statically and in the air, Irkut Corporation test pilots flying a series of high alpha manoeuvres demonstrating, to an extent, the designs super-manoeuvrability.

Deliveries of another batch of six Su-30SM's to the Russian Federation Air Force commenced in November 2013, and by early 2014 some 16 Su-30SM's were in service at Lipetsk and Domna. A further ten aircraft were delivered to Domna between the end of May and the end of September 2014, allowing formation of a second Su-30SM Squadron of the resident Air Regiment.

The production program called for production of 21 Su-30SM in 2014, some 17 having been delivered before the end of November that year, bringing to more than 30 the number of such aircraft delivered.

In January 2014 Su-30SM crews had commenced in-flight refueling training on the new multi-role fighters, operating from Lipetsk. Refuelling's were conducted in both day and night conditions at altitudes of 2000 m to 5000 m and speeds of 500 to 600 km/h, whereby the pilot would gradually move closer in to make contact with the refuelling drogue deployed by the tanker aircraft (zakontaktirovat barbell with cone sensor). The nighttime refuelling's were conducted courtesy of a supplemental lighting system installed on the Ilyushin Il-78 tanker aircraft.

In the first quarter of 2014, pilots newly graduated from the Krasnodar Military Aviation Institute commenced training on the Su-30SM at Lipetsk as the fleet began to establish itself in service.

Page 99-101: Aesthetically pleasing photographs of Su-30SM aircraft featuring the atmospheric phenomenon of twilight and a rainbow. JSC Corporation Irkut

The Su-30SM first appeared in the multi-tone dark scheme (top) before aircraft were delivered in the lighter multi-tone sky-blue scheme (above) more akin to the schemes worn by Su-27's. JSC Corporation Irkut

In early 2015, the Su-30SM unit at Domna, in company with Su-25SM ground attack aircraft, conducted a series of 250 kg bomb and missile firings against ground targets at a range facility in the territory of Buryatia in both day and night missions.

On 7 May 2015, a quartet of Su-30SM, in company with six Yak-130 advanced combat training aircraft of the 'Wings of Tauris' display team, participated in the fly past over Red Square, Moscow, to commemorate the 70th Anniversary of victory over Germany in the 'Great Patriotic War' – World War II. Two Su-30SM from Russian Naval Aviation participated in a fly past over Sevastopol, in the Russian Crimea, the Su-30SM's ever increasing public appearances signifying the type's importance to the re-equipment and modernisation of the Russian Federation Air Force, with around 100 such aircraft required in the shorter term.

As well as the Russian Federation Air Force, the Russian Navy looked to the Su-30SM to replace land based Su-27S air superiority fighters and Su-24M strike aircraft. To this end the Russian Navy ordered five Su-30SM in 2013, a contract for a further seven being signed at the 10th International Exhibition on Hydroaviation 2014 at Gidroaviasalon in Gelendzhik on 6 September 2014. Initially the Su-30SM was expected to replace Su-24M aircraft in service with the Russian Black Sea Fleet air arm. Later deliveries are expected to replace the Su-24 and Su-27 in the Baltic Fleet air arm.

Having flown during May and June 2014, three Su-30SM's, side codes 35, 36 and 37, were delivered to the Russian Navy on 19 July that year; being flown from Irkutsk to the Russian Federation Naval Aviation Combat Training Conversion Centre at Yeisk, Krasnodar Territory. A further order brought to 20 the number of Su-30SM's purchased for the Russian naval aviation with short term requirements being for up to 50 such aircraft.

The Russian Knights aerobatic display team conducted a series of familiarisation flights on the Su-30SM, including a number flown at MAKS-2013; the designs enhanced manoeuvrability being highly lauded by the team, it being announced in January 2016 that the team would re-equip with super manoeuvrable fighter aircraft, either a combination of the Su-35S and Su-30SM or perhaps the Su-30SM only.

Having a common defence treaty with Russia, the Su-30SM seemed like a logical choice to replace elements of the Kazakhstan fleet of Soviet era combat aircraft. In early 2015, a cadre of Kazakhstan Air Force air and ground personnel went to Irkutsk to commence training on the Su-30SM before returning to Kazakhstan on 4 March that year. Once Deliveries of aircraft commenced Kazakhstan Air Force pilots and ground personnel would be trained at Taldykorgan air base in Kazakhstan, the first Su-30SM for Kazakhstan arriving here on 17 April 2015; four such aircraft being delivered in April that month. As of early 2016, Kazakhstan has a requirement for around 20-24 Su-30SM.

Kazakhstan received its small fleet of four Su-30SM's in April 2015. JSC Corporation Irkut

6

ADVANCED WEAPONS PLATFORM

The Su-30MKI/MKM/MKI(A)/SM family of multirole 'super-manoeuvrable' combat aircraft can be armed with a wide diversity of air to air and air to surface weapons. There are slight differences in the armament suite of the respective operators of the various variants. For example, the Su-30MKI is the only variant currently projected to operate with the Brahmos air launched high-supersonic anti-ship missile. The Su-30SM, in service with the Russian Federation Air Force, is assumed to be capable of operating with the full spectrum of air to air and air to surface weapons operated by multi-role Su-27/35 variants in service with the Russian Federation Air Force. In the air to air role this would include semi-active radar, IR and anti-radiation variants of the R-27 medium-range air to air missile, the latter variant of which, as far as can be ascertained, is not in service with any other operator. As well as guided air to air and air to surface weapons, all operators can also employ a diversity of unguided air to surface weapons.

In Indian service the Su-30MKI was acquired as a replacement for a number of aircraft types including the MiG-27M 'Flogger', some of which apparently had a tactical nuclear role carrying a free fall atomic weapon, although it is unlikely that the Su-30MKI would adopt such a role, there being no indications in 2016 that such a role is contemplated.

In addition to externally carried ordnance all variants are armed with an internal GSh-301 30 mm cannon found in other members of the extended Su-27 family. This powerful weapon, housed in the starboard wing-root with 150 round of ammunition, can fire at a rate of between 1,500 and 1,800 rounds per minute, with a muzzle velocity of 870 meters per second. The cannon has a range out to around 1800 meters in the air to air role or up to 800 meters against surface targets. For air to air and air to ground missions the cannon is primarily a secondary weapon.

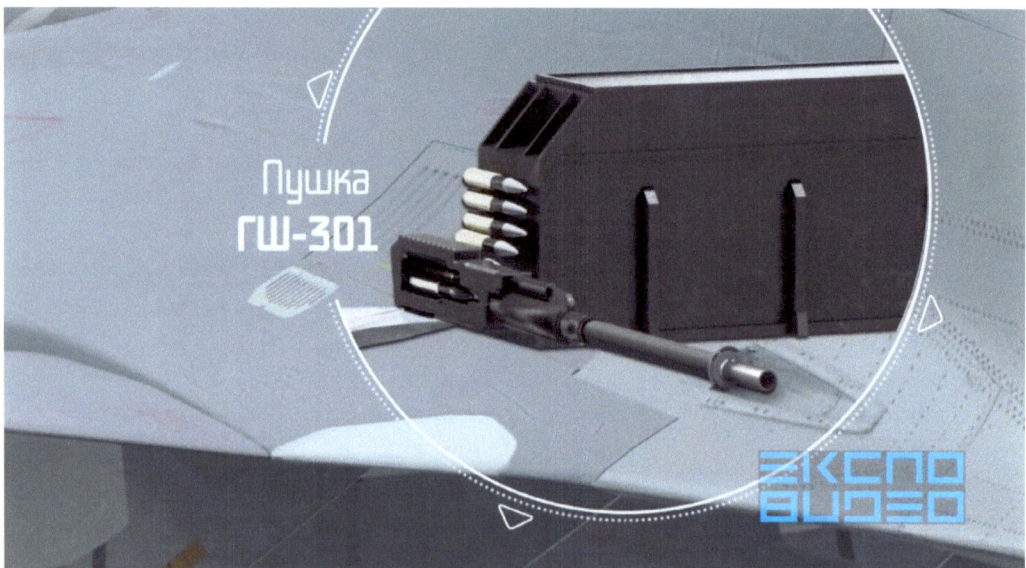

Top: Although optimised for the air combat role, the Su-30MKI series super-manoeuvrable fighter aircraft are true multirole combat aircraft capable of operating with a diversity of medium and short-range air to air missiles and guided and unguided air to surface munitions. This aircraft, the second Su-30MKI pre-production aircraft, is carrying a pair of R-73E infrared guided air to air missiles on the wingtip stations. JSC Corporation Irkut

Above: Graphic showing the fixed armament, a GSh-301 30 mm cannon with 150 round of ammunition. UAC

This Su-30MKI model is shown with a diversity of air to air and air to surface munitions: RVV-AE active radar guided medium range and R-73E infrared guided short range air to air missiles; X-59MK, X-31, X-29TE and X-29L air to surface missiles and a precision guided bomb on the centre fuselage stations. Author

In the air to air role the Su-30MKI series can be armed with the standard Russian medium and short-range air to air weapons; the Vympel (JSC Tactical Missiles Corporation) R-27ER1(R1), R-27ET1(T1), R-27EP1(P1), RVV-AE and R-73E (Note: Various in-house documentation refer to these weapons under differing but similar designations; for instance ER or RE. In the case of the ET1 and EP1 these are also sometimes referred to as ET/EP minus the 1. In Russian language the weapons are P-27, P-73 or K-27, K-73). As noted above, only the Su-30SM variant, in service with the Russian Federation Air Force, is expected to be armed with the R-27P1 (EP1) anti-radiation homing air to air missile designed to home in on opposing aircraft radar emitting in the forward hemisphere, a distinct advantage Russian fighter aircraft possess over their NATO opposite numbers.

Entering service in the mid-1980's as the primary air to air armament of the Su-27S, the R-27 medium-range missile variants in service in 2016 are more capable updates of the R-27, of which a whole family of variants was produced, including the R-27R, NATO reporting name AA-10 'Alamo' A with SARH (Semi-Active Radar Homing) guidance and the R-27T 'Alamo' B with IR (Infrared) guidance. Longer range variants were also developed, designated R-27ER1 for the SARH variant and R-27ET1 for the infrared guided variant. These missiles, 'Alamo' C and 'Alamo' D respectively, are fitted with a boost sustain motor to extend engagement range.

Graphics showing the Su-30MKI series armed with the maximum load of eight R-27P1(EP1) missiles (top) and two R-27T1 (ET1) infrared guided medium range air to air missiles (bottom). It should be noted that the P1(EP1) representation (top) most likely refers to the R-27R1 (ER1) semi-active radar guided variant and not the English language R-27P1(EP1) radiation homing missile. UAC

Up to eight R-27ER1(R1) missiles can be carried by the Su-30MKI series; two on the fuselage centre stations, one on each of the engine intake stations and one on each of the intermediate and inner wing stations. A maximum of two R-27ET1(T1) or R-27EP1(P1) missiles can be carried instead of the R-27ER1(R1); one on each of the intermediate wing stations. It should be noted that conflicting documentation states that up to eight R-27P1(EP1) radiation homing missiles can be carried, although two such missiles is more likely, this being the value for the Su-35S.

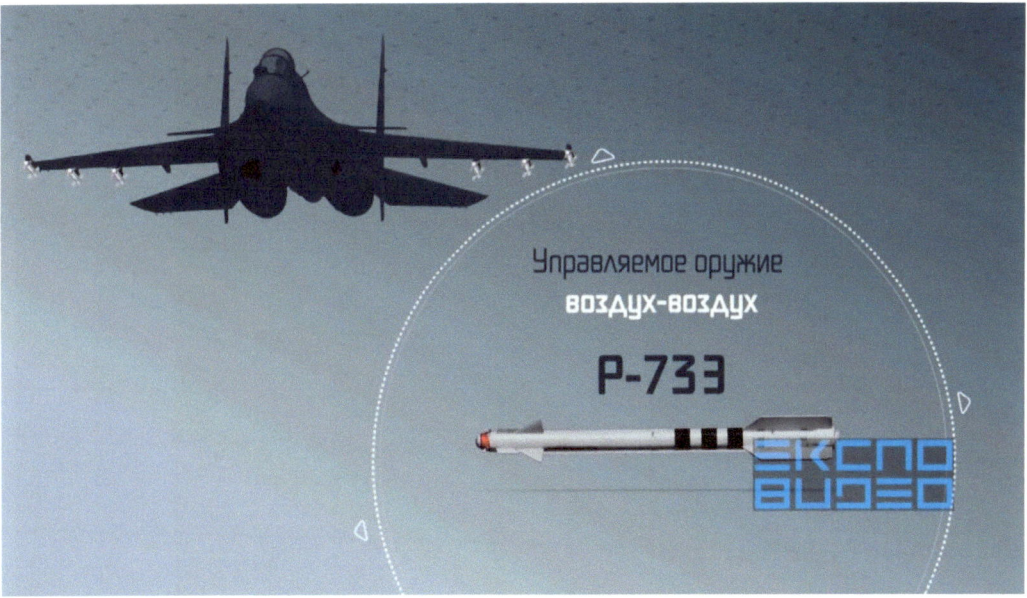

Top: This Russian Federation Air Force Su-30SM flying operational missions out of Hmeymim Air Base, Syria, is armed with R-27ER1 semi-active radar guided and R-73E short-range infrared guided air to air missiles. MODRF. Above: The Su-30MKI series can carry a maximum of six R-73E short-range infrared guided air to air missiles, one on each of the intermediate, outer and wingtip stations. UAC

Complementing the larger infrared guided R-27T1(ET1) is the smaller, shorter range, but highly agile, Vympel (JSC Tactical Missiles Corporation) R-73E (NATO reporting name AA-11 'Archer') infrared guided missile, six of which can be carried by the Su-30MKI series; one on each of the intermediate wing, one on each of the outer wing and one on each of the wingtip stations.

When it entered service in the 1980's, the R-73 was probably the most advanced short-range air to air missile in the world, being a generation ahead of the latest variants of the American AIM-9L/M Sidewinder or European Matra Magic 2 short-range infrared guided air to air missiles then arming NATO fighters. Only in the early 21st century did NATO field comparable systems in the shape of the MBDA (Matra British Aerospace Dynamics Alenia) ASRAAM (Advanced Short Range Air to Air Missile) and Raytheon AIM-9X Evolved Sidewinder.

The R-73 was developed with high agility as a design driver, augmented by the ability of the pilot of the Su-27 or MiG-29 fighters to cue the weapon to targets at up to 60° off-boresight via a HMSS (Helmet Mounted Sight System). High manoeuvrability was achieved by a combination of a number of factors, including four forward control fins, elevators attached to the rear fins, which are fixed, and deflector vanes positioned in the nozzle of the rocket engine.

The R-73E has a longer reach than most western equivalents such as the many AIM-9 variants; confirmed minimum engagement range against a tail-on target being 0.3 km with a maximum range of 30 km against a head-on target, with the capability to engage targets manoeuvring at up to 12 g.

The Su-30MKI can carry a maximum load of ten RVV-AE active radar guided air to air missiles, bestowing upon the aircraft an admirable feat of combat persistence. UAC

An RVV-AE test round is launched from what appears to be a Su-27UB test aircraft. KnAAPO

Up to ten Vympel (JSC Tactical Missiles Corporation) RVV-AE active radar guided medium range air to air missiles can be carried by the Su-30MKI family, eight on the same stations as those used for the carriage of the R-27ER1(R1) and an additional one on each of the outer wing stations. Development of this weapon apparently commenced in 1982, and the missile began entering limited service in the mid-1990's, certainly with trials units. Into the 21st century the weapon has been integrated with a number of aircraft types undergoing updates as well as new aircraft of the Su-27, Su-30, Su-34, Su-35S, MiG-29 and MiG-35 variants as well as the Sukhoi T-50 PAK FA fifth generation multi-role fighter aircraft. The weapon has also been exported to a number of customers, including India and Malaysia, and China also apparently purchased the missile for its Sukhoi Su-30MKK/MK2 multi-role fighters.

The RVV-AE has narrow-span wings of rectangular shape and four lattice control surfaces at the rear; among the benefits of this type of control surface being reduced flow-separation at high angle of attack. Like the US Raytheon AIM-120 AMRAAM (Advanced Medium Range Air to Air Missile) and the European MBDA MICA EM active radar guided missiles, the RVV-AE can be employed in a launch-and-forget mode and features a multi-stage guidance system that includes inertial in the initial phase with mid-course updates via an aircraft to missile datalink for long-range engagements, with active radar homing in the terminal phase of the engagement. The missiles on-board active-radar apparently has an acquisition-range of around 20 km.

Vympel noted that while the RVV-AE is heavier than the AIM-120A/C and MICA EM, the Russian missile has a longer range and better performance when engaging manoeuvring targets compared to its western rivals. The standard RVV-AE has a minimum engagement range of 0.3 km in the rear hemisphere and a maximum range of 80 km in the forward hemisphere, reaches a speed of Mach 4 and can engage targets manoeuvring at up to 12 g from 0.2 to 25 km altitude. The missile, which features an active-radar fuse for the 22.5 kg warhead, can also apparently be used in a 'self-defence' mode to intercept missiles launched at the mother aircraft.

Two views of a double RVV-AE launch from an Su-30SM. UAC

Although not currently specified in released documentation, it is expected that the RVV-MD and RVV-SD, respective replacements for the R-73E and RVV-AE will be integrated with Su-30 variants at a future date.

An evolution of the R-73E, the RVV-MD is a new generation highly agile infrared guided missile developed to arm the new generation of Russian $4^{th}++$ and 5th generation fighter aircraft. The JSC Tactical Missiles Corporation description states the "short range missile for close high manoeuvrable air combat provides hitting air targets (fighters, bombers, combat aircrafts, military aircrafts and helicopters), day and night, at all angles, on background of earth, under active enemy counteraction." The missile, which is powered by a single mode engine, features enhanced anti-jamming protection over its forebear, including optical jamming, and, as stated by the manufacturer, features "all angles passive infrared target homing (double range individual homing) with combined aero-gas dynamics control." The target is destroyed by a rod-shaped warhead activated by a laser non-contact sensor fuse in the RVV-MDL variant or a radio non-contact sensor in the RVV-MD. On Sukhoi and MiG fighter aircraft the weapon is carried on and launched from P-72-1D (P-72-1BD2) type rail tracked launcher.

The RVV-SD, developed by Vympel (JSC Tactical Missiles Corporation), is clearly an evolution of the RVV-AE incorporating a number of improvements over its forebear, with longer engagement range, increased engagement capability and enhanced resistance to electronic countermeasures. Tactical Missiles Corporation describes the missile as "intended for hitting air targets (fighters, bombers, attack aircraft, helicopters… cruise missiles) day and night, at all angles, under electronic countermeasures, on background of earth and water surfaces, including multichannel application 'fire-and-forget'". The missile, which is powered by a single mode rocket engine, incorporates inertial homing "with radar correction and active radar self-homing". The target is destroyed by a rod-shaped multi-charge warhead with detonation by laser non-contact target sensor. For external carriage on 4th, $4^{th}+$, $4^{th}++$ and 5th generation aircraft the missile is carried on and launched from the AKU-170E missile ejection launcher.

Vympel R-27 (JSC Tactical Missiles Corporation)

Propulsion: two mode solid propellant rocket motor
Length: 4.775 m for R-27ER1 and 4.49 m for R-27ET
Diameter: R-27ER1 and ET, 0.26 m at solid rocket section and 0.23 m at control unit section
Span: wing, 0.803 m and control plane 0.972 m
Launch weight: R-27ER1, 350 kg, R-27ET, 343 kg
Speed: Mach 4
Range: R-27ER1 – 60-62.5 km against fighter aircraft sized targets and up to 100 km against larger targets; R-27ET – 80 km in front hemisphere
Warhead: 39 kg expanding rod
Guidance: R-27R and R-27ER1 (SARH), R-27T and R-27ET (passive infrared)

> **Vympel R-73E (JSC Tactical Missiles Corporation)**
>
> **Propulsion:** solid propellant rocket motor
> **Length:** 2.9 m
> **Diameter:** 0.17 m
> **Span:** 0.51 m fin span and 0.38 m control plane span
> **Launch weight:** 105 kg
> **Range:** 30 km maximum head on and 0.3 km minimum tail on against up to 12 g manoeuvring targets
> **Engagement altitude:** from 0.02 to 20 km
> **Warhead:** 8 kg high explosive expanding rod
> **Guidance:** all-aspect passive infrared

> **Vympel RVV-AE (JSC Tactical Missiles Corporation)**
>
> **Propulsion:** solid propellant rocket motor
> **Length:** 3.6 m
> **Diameter:** 0.2 m
> **Wingspan:** 0.4 m
> **Control plane span:** 0.7 m in flight position
> **Launch weight:** 175 kg
> **Speed:** Mach 4 class
> **Range:** minimum 0.3 km in rear hemisphere and maximum 80 km in front hemisphere
> **Engagement altitude:** 0.2 to 25 km
> **Warhead:** 22.5 kg high explosive
> **Fuse:** active-radar
> **Guidance:** inertial, command and active-radar in the terminal phase

The Su-30MKI series can be armed with the Kh-31A (X-31A) anti-ship missile and the Kh-31P (X-31P) anti-radiation missile. A total of six Kh-31's can be carried, either all of the same variant or a mix of both variants. In the defence suppression role the six Kh-31P anti-radiation missile are carried on the following stations; one on each of the intake stations, one on each of the inner wing stations and one on each of the intermediate wing stations.

Documentation provided by JSC Tactical Missiles Corporation shows that the Kh-31P features "changeable passive radar homing heads… operating in corresponding frequency bands" allowing it to engage "modern continuous-wave and pulsed radar" systems employed by medium and long range surface to air missile systems. The missile can also engage other emitting radar systems not necessarily part of the air defence system. The homing head autonomously searches for and locks-on to a target, or, alternatively the launch aircraft sensors can hand down targeting information to the missile before it is launched from the AKU-58 airborne ejection unit.

Mock-up of an X-31 (Kh-31) air to surface missile (centre) exhibited below a Su-30MKK at the Paris Air Salon in 2001. Author

A modified variant of the missile, designated Kh-31PK, employs a larger warhead that is detonated by a proximity fuse. This variant retains the same operating parameters to those of the Kh-31P. The Kh-31PD is an evolution of the Kh-31P, range being increased from a maximum of 110 km to 250 km whilst carrying a more powerful warhead.

The Kh-31P, which has a launch weight of around 600 kg, is 4.7 m in length, 0.36 m in diameter and has a wing span of 0.914 m. The missile can be launched from altitudes of 100-15000 m at a carrier speed of Mach 0.65-Mach 1.25, after which it flies to targets between 15-110 km away (depending upon launch altitude) at speeds of 1000 m/s. The target is destroyed by an 87 kg high explosive fragmentation warhead.

As with the Kh-31P, the Su-30MKI series can carry up to six Kh-31A anti-ship missiles. Developed as a high-speed air launched anti-ship missile, the Kh-31A is designed to engage warships operating independently or as part of a larger integrated naval group. The missile, which has the same overall dimensions, similar launch weight, and identical launch parameters as the Kh-31P, can be launched from the carrier aircraft singly or in salvo in clear and adverse weather conditions, against background clutter in an active jamming environment. The missiles on-board active-radar homing head can designate targets in both pre-and-post launch modes and conduct target acquisition and selection, and, according to manufacturer documentation, determines "target coordinates (range, azimuth, elevation), generation of command signals", which are fed directly to the guidance system. The missile is carried on and launched from the AKU-58A ejection unit, cruising at a speed of 1000 m/s to targets 5-70 km distant (against a Destroyer size target) depending on launch altitude. The target is then destroyed or disabled by the 95 kg warhead.

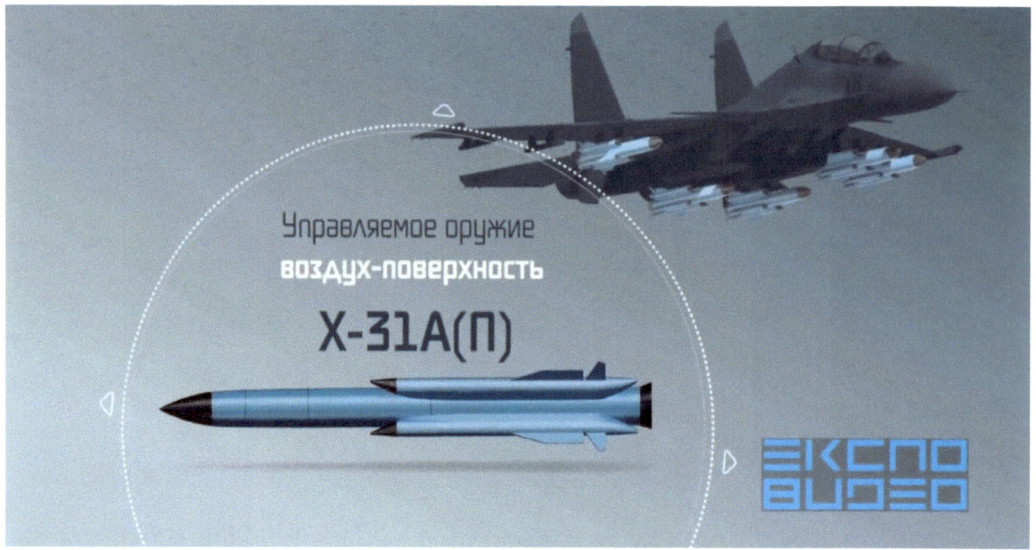

The Su-30MKI series can carry a maximum load of six X-31A or X-31P missiles (X-31A shown). UAC

The Kh-31AD is an evolution of the Kh-31A with many improvements including a 15% more powerful warhead and longer range; the latter being more than twice that of the Kh-31A.

Another anti-ship missile that can be integrated with the Su-30MK variants is the Kh-35E (X-35E), four of which can be carried; one on each of the inner and intermediate wing stations. This weapon, which is designed to destroy surface vessels, including warships displacing up to 5,000 tonnes, can be launched from warships (Uran-E ship-borne missile system), coastal missile batteries (Bal-E mobile coastal launch system) and aircraft launched. The aircraft launched missile has a length of 3.85 m, diameter 0.42 m, wing span 1.33 m and a launch weight of 520 kg.

Once launched from the mother aircraft, with maximum turn angle in horizontal plane after launch of ± 90°, the missile, which cruises at Mach 0.8, descends to an altitude of some 10-15 m above the sea surface, dropping to 4 m for the terminal phase of the flight, to strike targets up to 130 km distant in sea states up to 6 in an active electronic countermeasures environment; the ARGS-35E active radar seeker having an acquisition range of around 20 km, thereafter the target is locked-on and destroyed or disabled by the 145 kg high explosive penetrator warhead.

The Kh-35UE improves on the Kh-35E in a number of areas, including range, which is doubled from 130 km to 260 km, and an improved post-launch horizontal turn capability.

This Su-30MKI pre-production aircraft, Blue 05, is armed with an X-59ME (Kh-59ME) missile on the port inner wing station, the associated APK-9E guidance pod being located on the port side engine intake trunk station. JSC Corporation Irkut

The Kh-59ME (X-59ME) is an evolution of the Kh-59M (AS-13 'Kingbolt') introduced in the early 1990's. The missile (technical information pertains to the Kh-59M2E missile), which has a casing length of 5.7 m, casing diameter 0.38 m, wing span 1.3 m and a launch weight, stated by the manufacturer as being "up to 960 kg", can be launched from carrier aircraft flying at speeds of 600-1000 km/h and from altitudes of 0.2-5 km, the missile flying to targets out to 115-140 km (depending on launch parameters), cruising at Mach 0.72-Mach 0.88 at cruise altitudes of 0.007 km over sea or 0.05-1 km over land.

The Tactical Missiles Corporation description of the system reads "aircraft guided missile X-59M2E with translational command aiming system of the 'Ovod-ME' missile system provides hitting wide range of the ground and surface fixed targets with well known coordinates under conditions of limited visibility including night time."

The control system, as stated in manufacturer documentation, consists of an "aiming and automatic control system on the basis of inertial system unit + uncontrolled emergency jettison + low level television (imaging infrared)". The missile has a stated accuracy of 2 to 3 m in manual mode and 5 to 7 m in automatic mode, the target being destroyed by the penetrating warheads which is stated in JSC Tactical Missiles Corporation documentation can weigh "320" or "283" kg

This weapon is also employed by the Sukhoi Su-24M2 strike aircraft, guided by an APK-9 Ovod targeting pod carried by the launch aircraft with a datalink to the missile. Prior to missile launch, target coordinates are downloaded for the inertial guidance phase via the datalink. The Kh-59ME is also apparently integrated on the Su-34 'Fullback' intermediate range strike aircraft developed as a replacement for the Su-24 in Russian Federation Air Force service.

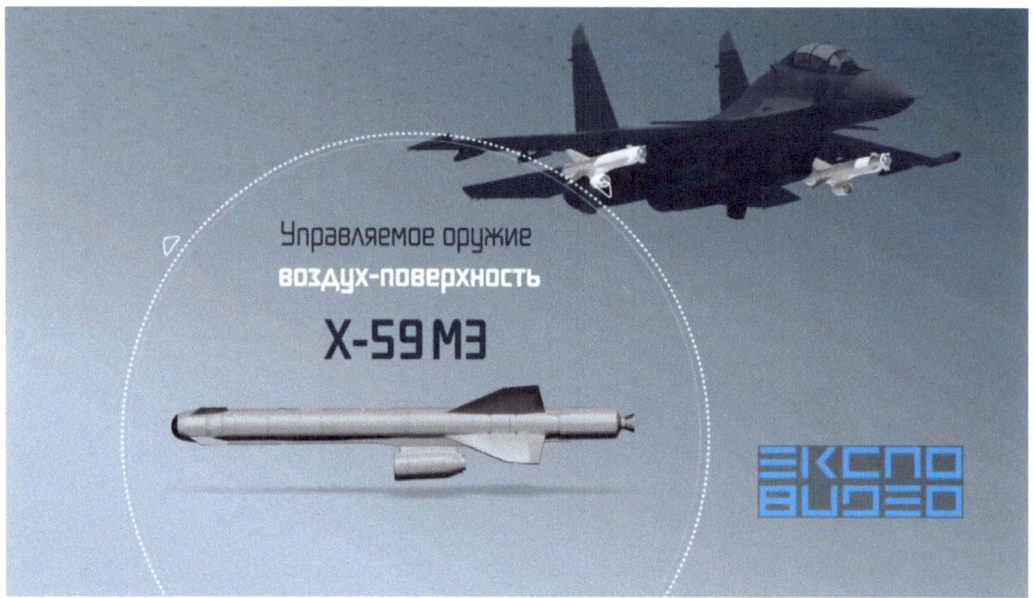

The Su-30MKI series can carry a maximum of two X-59ME air to surface missiles. UAC

Released Sukhoi documentation shows that the Kh-59MK (X-59MK) (AS-18 'Kazoo') is the standard long-range anti-ship strike weapon specified for the Su-30MKI series, while the Kh-59MK2 may be integrated for use against land targets. Four of these missiles can be carried; one on each of the inner wing stations and one on each of the intermediate wing stations, whereas only two of the Kh-59ME TV guided air to surface missile can be carried; one on each of the inner wing stations with an APK-9E guidance pod carried on the port engine intake station; the overall system known as the Ovod-ME as noted above.

Raduga unveiled the Kh-59MK, which is a development of the Kh-59M/ME, at the MAKS 2001 show in August 2001. The Kh-59MK, which has a length of 5.7 m, main body diameter (minus engine) of 0.38 m increasing to 0.42 m at the nose, wing span 1.3 m and a launch weight stated by the manufacturer as "not more than 930 kg", features an ARGS-58E active radar homing head claimed to be capable of detecting a destroyer size maritime target at a range of 25 km. The missile is powered by a low specific fuel consumption NPO Saturn 36MT turbofan engine, which extends the missiles range to 285 km when employed against a Destroyer size target, reducing to 145 km against smaller "boat size" targets. Minimum launch range is stated as 5.25 km. The Kh-59MK can be launched from the carrier aircraft when flying at speeds of Mach 0.5 to Mach 0.9 (600-1000 km/h) at altitudes of 0.2 to 11 km, the missile cruising to the target area at speeds of 900-1050 km/h at altitudes of 10-15 m over the sea, dropping to 4-7 m when in the terminal phase of the flight.

A maximum of four X-59MK air to surface missiles can be carried by the Su-30MKI series. NPO

A major improvement on the air to surface strike capability of the Su-30MKI will come with the introduction of the Brahmos Aerospace air launched variant of the Brahmos PJ-10 supersonic cruise missile, a Russo/Indian variant of the NPO Machinostroyenia Yakhont long-range anti-ship cruise missile.

The air launched variant of Brahmos is lighter than the two-stage surface/sub-surface launched variants. Modifications to the aerodynamic layout include additional fins at the rear of the missile to improve aerodynamic stability during the separation phase (when the missile drops away from the aircraft).

The missile is a true fire and forget weapon, a number of flight trajectories being possible as the missile cruises to the target area at high supersonic speed at cruise altitudes from sea level up to 15 km. Although often referred to as hypersonic, the missile is actually high supersonic, the target being attacked at speeds of Mach 3 at an altitude of around 10 m in the terminal phase. The surface launched variants have a flight range of 290 km, no figures so far having been released for the range of the air launched variant. The missile warhead weight is undisclosed, but the destructive power of the missile is vastly enhanced due to the high kinetic energy, equated to be around nine times that of a subsonic missile.

Integration of the missile on the Su-30MKI is being conducted under a partnership of Brahmos Aerospace, the Indian Air Force and JSC Sukhoi Design Bureau. Flight trials of the missile on the Su-30MKI was planned for late 2015, but appears to have been delayed until 2016.

Top: A single example of the large Brahmos Aerospace Brahmos Mach 3 air to surface missile can be carried by the Su-30MKI on the centre fuselage stations. UAC

Above: A Brahmos missile mock-up is shown on IAF Su-30MKI SB 023. As currently projected only the IAF will operate this weapon, which is derived from the surface launched Brahmos PJ-10. JSC Corporation Irkut

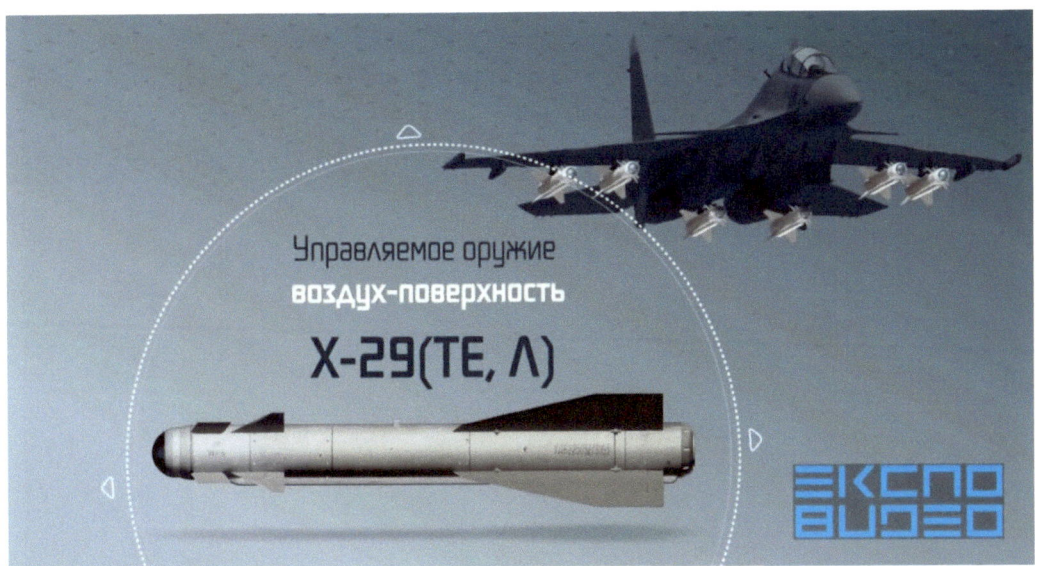

The Su-30MKI Series can carry a maximum load of six X-29TE/L short-range air to surface missiles. UAC

The Kh-29TE(L) are short range air to surface missiles, six of which can be carried by the Su-30MK family; one on each of the intake stations, one on each of the inner wing stations and one on each of the intermediate wing stations.

These weapons are designed for use against hardened targets such as large bridges, reinforced runways, industrial centres and aircraft housed in hardened aircraft shelters, and can also be employed effectively against surface vessels with a displacement up to 10,000 tons. The Kh-29 missiles, which are 3.9 m in length, 0.4 m diameter, 1.1 m wing span and have a launch weight of 690 kg for the Kh-29TE and 660 kg for the Kh-29L, are carried on and launched from AKU-58AE airborne ejector units; the Kh-29TE being guided to the target by a passive TV guidance system whilst the Kh-29L is fitted with a semi-active laser guidance system; the target being destroyed by the 320 kg high explosive penetrating warhead. JSC Tactical Missile Corporation documentation shows the missile to have a minimum engagement range of 3 km and a maximum engagement range of 20-30 km for the Kh-29TE (depending on launch altitude) and 10 km for the Kh-29L.

The Su-30MK family can also employ a number of guided and unguided bombs and rocket systems. Guided bombs include the KAB-500KR(OD) weapons, six of which can be carried on inner wing, intermediate wing and intake stations. A maximum of three of the larger KAB-1500KR(LG) weapons can be carried; one on the fuselage centre station and one on each of the inner wing stations.

Although not specified in released Sukhoi documentation, it is possible that the LGB-250 smart bomb will be integrated with Russian Federation Air Force Su-30SM strike fighters, six or perhaps eight (this latter number is specified for the Su-35S) could be carried.

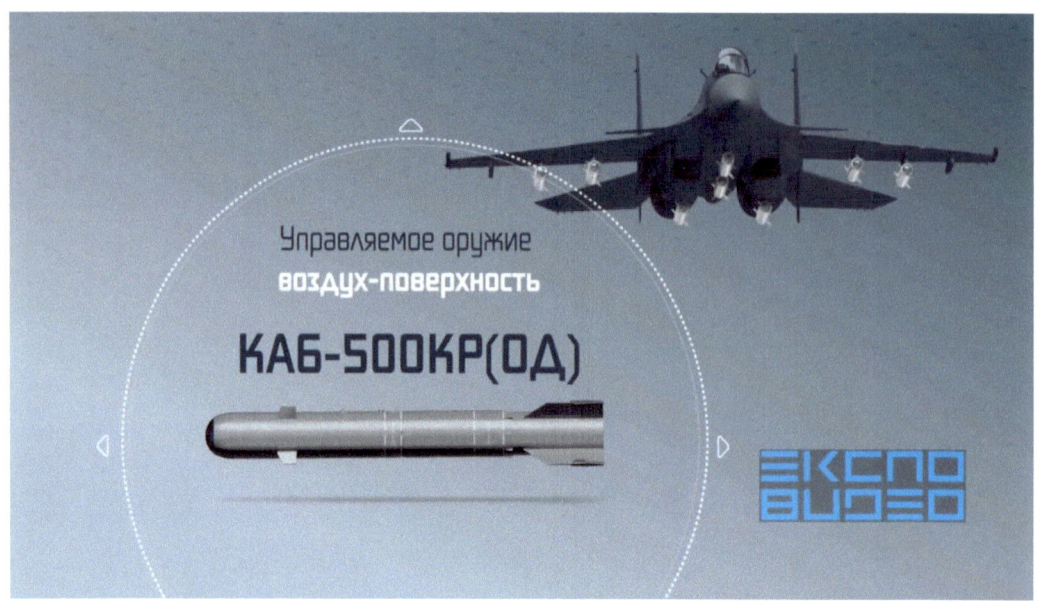

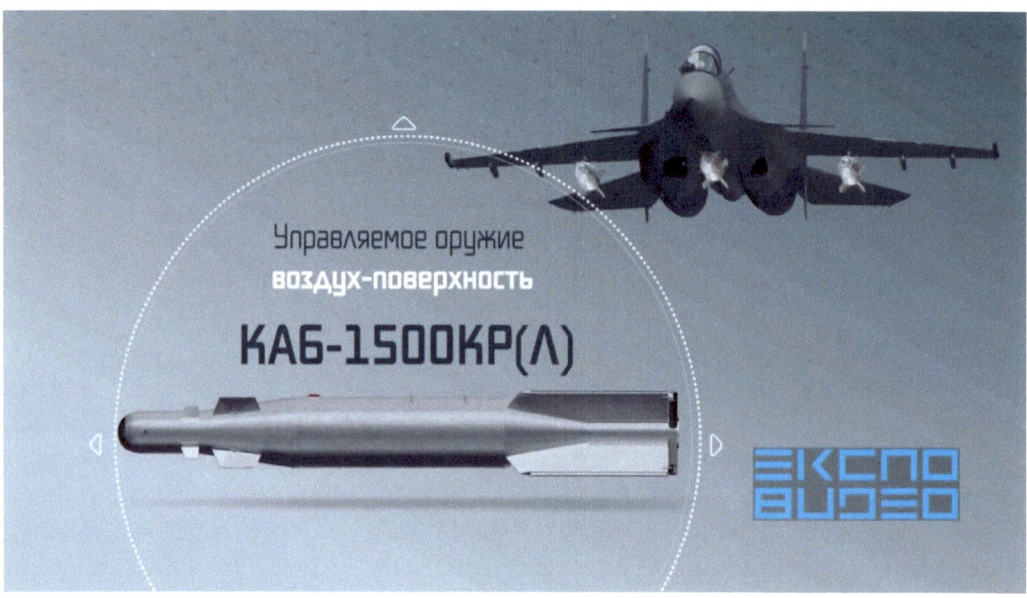

The Su-30MKI series can carry a maximum load of eight KAB-500 (top) or three KAB-1500 (bottom) precision guided bombs. UAC

The Su-30MK family can carry eight FAB-500 (ZB-500, RBK-500, BetAB-500) general purpose bombs; two on each of the intermediate wing stations, two on fuselage centre station and one on each of the intake stations. Twenty eight (some documentation suggests 32) of the smaller FAB-250 (OFAB-250-270) general purpose bombs can be carried in clusters on the same stations as used for the FAB-500 series. Alternatively the same stations can be used to carry up to thirty two OFAB-100-120 general purpose bombs.

The Su-30MK series can carry a maximum load of eight FAB-500 (ZB-500, RBK-500, BetAB-500) general purpose bombs (top), or 32 FAB-250/100 bombs (centre). Unguided rockets can include four B-8M-1 rocket pods (above). UAC

Unguided rockets can include up to four B-8M-1 rocket pods; two on each of the intermediate wing stations or four smaller B-13L rocket pods can be carried on the same stations. Another alternative is four S-25, S-250OFM-PU rockets which are carried on the same stations as the B-8M-1 and B-13L. KnAAPO documentation shows that up to eight of the P-50T weapons can be carried on the intermediate wing stations (two each), fuselage centre station and engine intake stations of the Su-30MK2, this likely being the same load out for the Su-30MKI series.

	KAB-500Kr	KAB-500-OD	KAB-1500Kr
Launch weight:	520 kg	370 kg	1525 kg
Warhead weight:	380 kg	250 kg	1170 kg
High explosive:	100 kg	250 kg	440 kg
Length:	3.05 m	3.05 m	4.63 m
Diameter:	0.35 m	0.35 m	0.58 m
Empennage:	0.75 m	0.75 m	0.85 m (folded)
Release altitude:	0.5-5 km	0.5-5 km	1-8 km
Carrier speed:	550-1100 km/h	550-1100 km/h	550-1100 km/h
Root mean Square deviation:	4…7 m	4…7 m	4…7 m
Warhead type:	concrete piercing (high explosive penetrator)	high explosive fuel air	high explosive

	KAB-1500LG-PrE	KAB-1500LG-F-E	KAB-1500LG-OD-E
Launch weight:	1525 kg	1525 kg	1450 kg
Warhead weight:	1120 kg	1120 kg	1170 kg
High explosive:	210 kg	440 kg	650 kg
Length:	4.28 m	4.28 m	4.24 m
Diameter:	0.58 m	0.58 m	0.58 m
Wingspan:	0.85 m (retracted) 1.3 m (extended)	0.85 m (retracted) 1.3 m (extended)	0.85m (retracted) 1.3 m (extended)
Release altitude:	1-8 km	1-8 km	1-10 km
Aircraft drop speed:	550-1100 km/h	550-1100 km/h	550-1100 km/h
Aiming accuracy:	4-7 m	4-7 m	4-7 m
Warhead:	penetrator	high explosive	fuel air explosive
Fusing:	contact with three types of delay	contact with three types of delay	direct-action contact

7

RUSSIAN AEROSPACE GROUP SU-30SM OPERATIONS OVER SYRIA

On 30 September 2015, the Russian Aerospace Forces detachment based at Hmeymim air base in the Syrian Arab Republic commenced bombing operations against "ISIS" and a number of other terrorist and so called moderate opposition groups fighting against Syrian government forces. This immediately became a source of tension between Russian and NATO nations as many of the opposition groups were supported by the western powers who hoped to exert their influence over that oil producing part of the Middle East by toppling the Syrian President. As well as targeting tactical targets, the Russian Aerospace Group, which consisted of Su-24M and Su-34 strike aircraft, Su-25SM ground attack aircraft and a four strong detachment of Su-30SM multirole fighters, periodically backed up by bombing and cruise missile launch missions of Russia's strategic aviation forces – Tu-22M3, Tu-95MS and Tu-160 strategic bombers and cruise missiles launched by Russian Navy surface vessels in the Caspian Sea and a Submarine in the Mediterranean Sea. The Russian assault also began targeting the huge volumes of illegal oil, which the Russian Federation Ministry of Defence pointed out was brazenly being transported and sold through Turkey, becoming a major source of revenue for ISIS. This, perhaps, became the main source of tension between Russia and Turkey.

By January 2016, the four strong Su-30SM detachment had flown hundreds of sorties of the overall 5,000 or so flown by the Russian Aerospace Group operating out of Hmeymim. The Su-30SM sorties consisted of air to ground and air defence, the latter role assuming greater importance from late November 2015, following the shooting down of a Su-24 strike aircraft by Turkish F-16 fighter aircraft over Northern Syria, causing sub-surface tension within the NATO alliance. From this point Russian strike aircraft operating near the Turkish border were escorted by Su-30SM's, as were strategic bombers operating over Syria from bases within Russia.

In theory there should have been no air threat to Russian aircraft operating over Syria, but Russian mistrust of NATO, meant that the small Su-30SM detachment of four aircraft, Red 26, 27, 28 and 29, were primarily tasked with an air to air role armed with R-27ER1 SARH (Semi-Active Radar Homing) and R-73E short-range IR (Infrared) guided air to air missiles. The standard air defense load for operations over Syria was typically two or sometimes four R-27ER1 SARH and two R-73E IR homing missiles, it being of interest to note that they aircraft did not operate with RVV-AE active radar guided air to air missiles, suggesting that the R-27ER1 is favoured over the RVV-AE or that the latter weapon, although undoubtedly available in Russia, is not in full operational service with Russian Federation Air Force Squadrons, or at least not yet operational with the Su-30SM fleet.

Limited air to surface operations were carried out against ground targets, air to surface ordnance usually being restricted to a few unguided bombs carried on the intake trunk weapon stations, these typically being OFAB-250-270 class weapons. Some aircraft were equipped with wingtip mounted EW (Electronic Warfare) sensor pods, the L175U Khibiny-U self-defence system optimised for the Su-30SM, enhancing the overall strike package EW defense against potential NATO jamming.

While encounters with the US-led coalition aircraft occurred periodically, most were of a non-threatening nature on either side, although there were a few occasion, prior to flight safety regulations being fully imposed by both sides that were cause for concern. On one such occasion on 10 October 2015, a Su-30SM was escorting a group of Russian strike aircraft when, according to the Russian Defence Ministry, the "radar warning receiver system of the Russian jets detected radio impulses of an unidentified aircraft. The Russian aircraft (Su-30SM) reached the distance of about two-three kilometers. This caused some concern within the US-led coalition, the Russian Defence Ministry stating that "there was no intention to scare anybody. The Russian pilot did that just to identify the aircraft." Following the incident the Su-30SM, having made the point that the Russians were capable of defending the strike package, returned to said strike package and continued with the escort mission.

This was one of several incidents, the Russians pointing out that they often identified US combat aircraft along with UAV (Uninhabited Air Vehicles), releasing several videos showing the latter being intercepted in a non-hostile manner.

From early in the mission, Russian mistrust of NATO nations seemed justified as Turkey in particular became threatening in its accusations of Russian violations of its airspace, which although several most probably did occur as certain targets were close to the Syrian/Turkish border, were of only a few seconds duration as Su-24M strike aircraft in particular, were engaging targets claimed to be ISIS and other terrorist groups, which it claimed were freely crossing into Syria from Turkey.

Tensions between Turkey and Russia in regards to Russian air operations came to a climax on 24 November 2015 when, as noted above, Turkish F-16's shot down a Russian Su-24 which crashed about five miles inside Syrian territory. From that date the Su-30SM detachment began flying escort missions for Russian strike aircraft operating near the Turkish border, it being made clear that any Turkish or other NATO air interference with the Russian missions would result in these aircraft being engaged. The success of the detachment in the air to air role may be summed up in the fact that, despite Turkish insistence that Russian violations of its air space continued, no further attempts were made by Turkey to interfere with the Russian operations.

Su-30 Super-Manoeuvrable Family

137

Page 127-142: Ensemble of photographs of the four strong Su-30SM detachment at Hmeymin Air Base, Syrian Arab Republic. Offensive and defensive air operations commenced on 30 September 2015. Above: from late November Russia positioned air defence systems including S-400 Triumph long-range surface to air missiles at Hmeymin to counter the threat from NATO aircraft. MODRF

8

SUPER-MANOEUVRABILITY – 4TH+/4TH++/5TH GENERATION NECESSITY OR LUXURY?

It is generally accepted that the Su-30MKI got the better of aircraft in the F-15C and Eurofighter Typhoon class in mock combats conducted during international exercises and bilateral dissimilar air combat training. Against the stable of western 5th generation fighters, the Lockheed Martin F-22 Raptor and F-35 Lightning II, the Su-30MKI series would certainly outperform the F-35 in the accepted physical traits of a fighter aircraft: speed, climb and manoeuvrability; certainly in the latter trait having a clear edge over not only the F-35, but also the F-22, particularly in the slow-speed high alpha flight regime. However, it is not the intention in this volume to conduct an in depth analysis of these aircraft pitted against each other in an air combat environment as such an exercise would be fraught with difficulties in the space available, particularly when force multipliers such as AWACS (Airborne Warning and Control) systems are considered.

Although no in-depth analysis would be reliable at this time, it is possible to give an overview of potential operational scenarios that could evolve in the event that the Su-30MKI series encountered either of the western 5th generation fighter aircraft in a hostile environment. Much of the following text on operational scenarios is adapted from text in the volume 'Sukhoi Su-35S, Russia's Super-Manoeuvrability Fighter' by the author, first published in 2015. While this text referred to the Su-35S, it remains applicable to the Su-30MKI series, although it should be stated that the Su-35S has a higher performance in areas such as speed, climb and thrust to weight ratio, the difference in speed being in the order of Mach 0.25 at altitude in the Su-35S favour. In regards to fire control systems, the Tikhomirov NIIP IRBIS-E of the Su-35S is superior to the Bars system installed in the Su-30MKI series. The OLS-35 optical location system installed in the Su-35S is also more advanced that the system installed in the Su-30MKI series, both units being very capable systems for detecting airborne and surface targets.

The expression often used by western fighter aircraft manufacturers when referring to the capability of fifth generation 'stealth' aircraft such as the F-22A, is 'first look, first shot, first kill', or the shortened variant of the expression used by Northrop Grumman, designer of the F-22A's AN/APG-77 AESA (Active-Electronically Scanned Array), "first look, first kill". These phrases in effect sum up the USAF public view of modern air to air combat; being to detect and engage the enemy at long/medium range and shoot him down before he can bring his weapons to bear and return fire. The basis for this philosophical viewpoint is the F-22A's excellent low-observable qualities that far exceed those of any other in-service air superiority fighter aircraft, combined with the highly capable AN/APG-77 radar fire control system which, as stated by the manufacturer, is designed to "exhibit a very low radar cross section", that, in 2015, is probably the most capable radar system installed in an air superiority aircraft, with the exception of detection range in which it appears to be inferior to the IRBIS-E of the Su-35S. That said, although being dubbed low-probability of intercept, the APG-77, like all fighter aircraft radar systems (all radar –radio direction finding systems emit detectable radio emissions – electromagnetic radiation without exception), can be and will be detected by an adversary in a modern 4+, 4++ or 5th generation fighter aircraft, although at what range remains unclear. The range at which the APG-77 is detected is extremely unlikely to be less than the typical engagement range for an AIM-120 AMRAAM shot of well under 20 miles.

Against a Su-30MKI series aircraft in the frontal hemisphere the F-22A would, in all probability, be detected by the formers Optical Location System through the formers thermal radiation (infrared – heat) signature, which, although vastly reduced over that of 4th generation aircraft, is still a considerable heat source, particularly as the F-22A accelerates to gain launch energy for its AMRAAM's. There is simply no getting around the physics: acceleration = air friction resulting in increased amount of thermal energy. Even without this additional thermal energy generated by the increased friction of acceleration, all known matter emits thermal radiation through molecular movement. As denoted by the third law of thermodynamics, molecular movement does not stop unless matter is reduced to a temperature of absolute zero, which stands at 0° kelvin – a more than chilly -273° C. To reduce matter, that makes up all physical things, to such temperatures would render the aircraft to a frozen state and, ipso facto, incapable of flight. Is it possible to design an aircraft that does not emit a detectable thermal signature? Certainly not with current technology levels; all matter in molecular motion has a thermal radiation signature whether it is a rock on the ground or a man-made structure such as an aircraft at rest on the ground or flying at Mach 2 at altitude. The RAM (Radar Absorbent Materials) that reduce the F-22 or F-35 detectable footprint in the electromagnetic spectrum actually increase air friction thereby increasing the aircraft thermal radiation footprint in the infrared spectrum, the OLS, thus being the ideal counter to 5th generation stealth aircraft.

While the 'first look, first shot, first kill' philosophy may have some basis against obsolete aircraft equipped with obsolete systems, against an opponent fielding modern aircraft equipped with modern systems in the class of the Su-30MKI series, such a philosophy may well be doomed to failure. Even if, as would be expected, an

F-22A detected the Su-30MKI series first, in regards to the radar detection, (first look) and launched its AMRAAM's (first shot), these missiles will be very hard pushed to kill the Su-30MKI series with its high speed, excess power, extensive countermeasures and super-manoeuvrability designed to evade modern air to air missiles. Such super-manoeuvrability could be used to effectively defeat AMRAAM, particularly as the weapon loses kinetic energy in the end game of the engagement.

If the F-22A, after firing missing with its AMRAAMs, turns away, then it has failed in the mission, conceding the airspace to the Su-30MKI series. If the F-22A continues toward the oncoming Su-30MKI series then it will not only be fast approaching the close combat arena where the Russian aircraft, with its super-manoeuvrability, excels, it will also, having been detected by the oncoming Su-30MKI Series, have to avoid the latter's medium range counter fire of RVV-AE active radar guided missiles as well as the long/medium range radar guided R-27ER1 and infrared guided R-27ET1 missiles; this of course being the case only if the Su-30MKI series detects the on-coming F-22 in time to launch its medium-range counter fire before having to manoeuvre violently to avoid the on-coming AMRAAM missiles. Another headache for the F-22A pilot would be the R-27EP1 long/medium range missile designed to home in on the radar emissions of enemy aircraft that may well form part of the armoury of the Russian Federation Air Force Su-30SM.

If an aircraft in the class of the F-35 turns away after missing the Su-30MKI series with its AMRAAM's it will, in all probability, find itself in the unenviable situation of being at the disadvantage of height and certainly at a disadvantage of speed (at altitude in the order of 400 km/h slower than the Su-30MKI series), whereby it could not escape from a Su-30MKI series intent on bringing the F-35 to combat.

As previously stated, 'first look, first shot, first kill' is merely a marketing and publicity gimmick, the USAF no doubt under no illusion that such scenarios would be typical of air combat against a major military power equipped with modern air superiority aircraft and systems such as a 21st century resurgent Russia. The simple fact is that if it was genuinely thought that aircraft like the F-22A could simply pluck enemy aircraft from the sky without ever having to come into close range then their armament would need consist only of medium range missiles like AMRAAM (which can also be used at closer ranges), there being no need for close range (so called dogfighting) IR guided weapons, or indeed a cannon armament. Regardless of stealth features, the benefits of which become a liability when an engagement comes down to close-range, the F-22A and F-35A retain the weapons for close-range combat in the form of the AIM-9X Sidewinder infrared guided air to air missile and the internal cannon. This fact alone clearly demonstrates that the USAF does not expect that the F-22A will always be able to engage an enemy only at medium ranges and outwards.

It also has to be considered that radar guided air to air missiles launched from medium ranges; even from around fourteen or fifteen miles from the target, have a very poor probability of hitting a modern 4+, 4++ or 5th generation air superiority fighter actively trying to evade such missiles, the F-22A therefore having to close the range for another missile shot whereby the missile will have more kinetic energy in the end game with a greater chance of success. The alternative is to turn away, using speed to avoid being drawn into a close range fight; for the F-35 pilot this may well be to court disaster, for, as previously stated, that design lacks the speed to escape an aircraft in the class of the Su-3MKI series, which would also most probably be operating with a height advantage.

As the opposing forces close on each other in a head on engagement the stealth advantage of the F-22 or F-35 has been nullified, the design of such aircraft now proving to be a handicap as the aircraft enter a close combat environment, both losing speed, possibly passing as they manoeuvre, finding it harder to position themselves advantageously for a missile shot; the 'super-manoeuvrability' of the Su-30MKI, however, allowing that aircraft to completely turn around more or less on its axis within about three seconds with a manoeuvre such as a 'controlled flat spin' which could follow for example a 'kulbit' manoeuvre to bleed off airspeed, for another missile shot, the opponent aircraft, be it an F-22A or an F-35, being in the unfortunate position whereby it cannot reciprocate, thereby becoming the quarry instead of the hunter.

As noted above, there are of course many other factors for a real world situation such as aircraft numbers on either side, force multipliers such as AWACS, weapons carried, countermeasures, of which 'super-manoeuvrability can be considered one, fuel load remaining at the commencement of the engagement etc. However, it is clear that while a 5th generation air superiority fighter like the F-22A has obvious certain advantages over the 4+ Su-30MKI series, the Russian fighter has obvious certain advantages over its western counterparts, particularly when the engagement comes down to close-range.

Detractors of the need for super-manoeuvrability in an air superiority aircraft should consider this point: super-manoeuvrability is an additional weapon/countermeasure in the aircraft arsenal; it does not come at the sacrifice of other air combat traits such as speed, altitude and weapon carrying ability in the way a pure stealth driven design sacrifices much of what is considered essential traits for an air combat fighter.

The Su-30MKI series builds on the already impressive manoeuvring capabilities of previous generations of the extended Su-27/30 family of combat aircraft. From their earliest public demonstrations in the late 1980's, it was clear that the basic Su-27 air superiority fighter possessed manoeuvring capabilities that far exceeded those of its western counterparts in most areas. Having previously demonstrated the 'Cobra' and 'Hook' manoeuvres, which clearly demonstrated advances in extreme incidence flight in an operational aircraft - the Su-27S, the Russians again stole a march on western fighter manufacturers in 1996, by demonstrating such manoeuvres as the 'Kulbit' with the Su-37MR equipped with thrust vector control for its engine nozzles.

The 'Kulbit' manoeuvre is basically a 'Cobra' like manoeuvre that, following the high speed run and rapid pitch upwards to the vertical, and often beyond, of the 'Cobra', rather than bringing the nose back down as in the 'Cobra', the aircraft continues on through the vertical to complete a full rotation around the aircraft lateral axis; in effect an airborne somersault. Another 'Cobra' like manoeuvre saw the aircraft perform a rapid pitch up to around 130°, maintaining this attitude for some

2-3 seconds whilst rapidly bleeding-off airspeed. The pilot then used vectored-thrust, pitching the aircraft nose forward before recovering into a dive. Like the 'Cobra' and 'Hook' beforehand, some observers questioned the operational value of such manoeuvres, although the potential in close air combat, particularly in evasion of missile shots, appeared obvious, although only as a last resort as the aircraft inevitably loses kinetic energy very rapidly. That said, the Su-30MKI series, and in particular the Su-35S, possess excellent acceleration, being capable of regaining speed very quickly.

The 'Bell' manoeuvre demonstrated by the Su-35S could be described as a 'Cobra' manoeuvre whereby the aircraft, keeping its nose towards the vertical, retains its altitude in the sky without slowly descending tail first; the aircraft in effect appearing to more or less stand still with its nose more or less at the vertical, around 90° (although often pulling over to around 100°), while maintaining some forward motion. Coming out of the vertical the pilot initiates a 180° turn, completely reversing the aircraft original course prior to the commencement of the manoeuvre. When these manoeuvres are conducted by the Su-30MKI series, these aircraft inevitably begin the so called 'Tail Slide' as the aircraft lacks the power to hold its altitude in the sky. The Su-35S, with its 117S engines in afterburner, can hold its altitude and maintain forward flight at speeds of between 120-140 km/h during such manoeuvres.

Another manoeuvre conducted by the Su-30MKI series and the Su-35S is a controlled flat spin (also demonstrated by the PAK FA/T-50 5th generation fighter) whereby the pilot retains full control of the aircraft as it conducts a rotating descent.

There will, of course, be additional extreme agility manoeuvres that may come to light; adding to the well-known Pugachev's 'Cobra', 'Spatial barrel', 'Kulbit' style somersaults, the 'Bell, and the controlled 'Flat spin'. The rapid deceleration caused by many of these extreme manoeuvres may cause a radar to break lock, which would be extremely useful in avoiding radar guided missiles. Of course, there are other manoeuvres that make the Su-30MKI series and the Su-35S very unpredictable in their flight pattern, an environment that is not ideal for air to air missiles to achieve a successful engagement.

Exercise Coup Taufan, held in Malaysia in 2014, included a number of USAF and RMAF aircraft types: BAE Systems Hawk, MiG-29N, Su-30MKM, F-15C and the F-22 making its Far East exercise debut. The various aircraft types were involved in a series of exercise scenarios including dissimilar air combat. As with the mock combat training of Indian Su-30MKI's against various US and European aircraft types, there has been rumour and speculation that the Su-30MKM's proved a severe problem for the F-22, the latter types low-observability traits proving less effective than would have been hoped. However, there have been no officially sanctioned reports as to the results of any such engagements released by either the USAF or RMAF, therefore such unofficial reports should be viewed with a degree of caution until conclusive data emerges proving or disproving them.

Page 148-150: Sequence of graphics showing the Su-30SM being put through a series of manoeuvres commencing with a 'Kulbit' and ending with a 'controlled flat spin'. UAC

APPENDICES

APPENDIX 1

PROTOTYPE and PRE-PRODUCTION AIRCRAFT		
	First Flight	Last flight
Prototypes		
T-10PMK-1	1 July 1997	Lost in a crash in June 1999
T-10PMK-6	23 March 1998	
Pre-production		
Code 02, 04, 05 (also possibly code 03)	26 November 2000	

Note: The T-10P-MK-1 was converted from the Su-30M, Blue 56, and the T-10PMK-6 was converted from the T-10PU-6 (a Su-27UB)

APPENDIX II

OPERATORS							
	India	Malaysia	Algeria	Russia	Kazakhstan	Angola	Iraq
Su-30K	18					12	6
Su-30MKI	272						
Su-30MKM		18					
Su-30MKI(A)			44				
Su-30SM				110	4		

Note: The Su-30SM is operated by the Russian Federation Air Force (Aerospace Forces) 60 and the Russian Naval Air Arm 20. Kazakhstan apparently has a requirement for up to 24 Su-30SM including the four already delivered in 2015. A further 30 Su-30SM were ordered for the Russian Federation Air Force on 4 April 2016, this figure being included in the table above.

Note 2: Angola purchased 12 of the surplus Su-30K's returned to Russia by India in 2007, the remaining six being delivered to Iraq in 2015.

Note 3: In addition to the aircraft numbers mentioned above there was also the single Su-30MK demonstrator, side code 603 as well as the Su-30M's built for the Russian domestic market, one of these serving as the Su-30KN demonstrator and one serving as the Su-30I-1 (Su-30MKI) prototype.

APPENDIX III

Su-30MKI series Specification (JSC/Sukhoi/ JSC Corporation Irkut/UAC data)

Powerplant: two x AL-31FP bypass turbofan engines each rated at 12500 kgf with afterburner
Length: 21.9 m
Height: 6.4 m
Wing span: 14.7 m
Normal Take-off weight: 24900 kg (figures for Su-30MK) configured with 2 x R-27R1, 2 x R-73E air to air missiles and 5720 kg of fuel
Maximum take-off weight: 34000 kg (Irkut values) and 34500 kg (Sukhoi values; these possibly relating to the Su-30MK2). Sukhoi provides a value of 38000 kg absolute limit which does not appear to be replicated by Irkut confirming that this is representative only of the Su-30MK2 which is structurally distinct from that of the Su-30MKI series
Landing weight: 23600 kg normal and 30000 kg maximum
Internal fuel load: 5270 kg normal and 9400 kg maximum according to values provided by Irkut. Conflicting documentation from Sukhoi states 9640 kg maximum
Fuel specific gravity: 0.0785 g/cc. cm
Maximum level speed: 1350 km/h at sea level, 2100 km/h at high altitude for Su-30MKI series and 1400 km/h at sea level and 2120 km/h at altitude for Su-30MK2 series
Maximum Mach number at high altitudes: 1.9 for Su-30MKI series and Mach 2 for Su-30MK2 series
Ceiling: 17300 m without external stores
Range with maximum fuel load: when expending 2 x R-27R1 and 2 x R-73E air to air missiles "at half distance", 1270 km at sea level, 3000 km at altitude without in-flight refuelling and 5200 km with one in-flight refuelling (figures for the Su-30MK2 are 3000 km and 5600 km respectively for the latter two values)
Maximum airborne time: pilot dependant, but generally stated as 10 hours
In-flight refuelling system: 100 l/m at "maximum flow rate (at entry pressure of 3.5 kg/cm^2)
Take-off run: 550 m at normal take-off weight in afterburner
Landing roll: 750 m at normal landing weight with deployment of a braking parachute
Load limit: 9 g.
Crew: 2
Fixed armament: GSh-301 30 mm cannon housed in starboard wing root with 150 rounds of ammunition
Maximum external stores load: 8000 kg carried on twelve external stations. Can include various combinations of R-27ER1(R1), R-27ET1(T1), R-27EP1, RVV-AE, R-73E air to air missiles, Kh-29TE(L), Kh-31P(A), Kh-35E and Kh-59ME/MK air to surface missiles, KAB-500Kr(OD) and KAB-1500Kr(LG) guided bombs and various combinations of unguided bombs and rockets
Service life: 3000 hours
Time to first overhaul: 1500 hours
Engine and outboard accessory gearbox life: 500 hours to first overhaul and 1500 hours service life

APPENDIX IV

Su-27UB (JSC Sukhoi Design Bureau data)

Powerplant: 2 x AL-31F afterburning turbofan engines each rated at 12500 kgf -2% in afterburner and 7670 kgf in full military power +/-2%
Length: 21.9 m
Wingspan: 14.7 m
Height: 6.4 m
Normal take-off weight: 23900 kg with 2 x R-27R1 and 2 x R-73E missiles and 5270 kg of fuel
Maximum take-off weight: 33000 kg
Maximum internal fuel load: 9400 kg
Maximum Mach number: 2.0
Ceiling: 17.5 km in clean configuration
Operational range configured with 2 x R-27R1 and 2 x R-73E air to air missiles when the missiles are launched at "half distance": 1270 km at sea level and 3000 km at altitude
Take-off run: 550 m at normal take-off weight
Landing run with braking parachute: 670 m at normal landing weight
Crew: 2

Su-27S (Specification is generally the same as Su-27UB except in the following)

Height: 5.9 m
Normal take-off weight: 23400 kg with 2 x R-27R1 and 2 x R-73E missiles and 5270 kg of fuel
Maximum take-off weight: 30450 kg
Maximum landing weight: 23000 kg
Maximum speed at sea level: 1400 km in clean configuration
Maximum Mach number: 2.35
Ceiling: 18.5 km in clean configuration
Operational range configured with 2 x R-27R1 and 2 x R-73E air to air missiles when the missiles are launched at "half distance": 1340 km at sea level and 3530 km at altitude
Take-off run: 450 m at normal take-off weight
Landing run with braking parachute: 620 m at normal landing weight
Load limit: 9 g
Crew: 1

GLOSSARY

ACS	Automatic Control System
AESA	Active Electronically Scanned Array
AIM	Airborne Interception Missile
AMRAAM	Advanced Medium Range Air to Air Missile
AoA	Angle of Attack
ASRAAM	Advanced Short-Range Air to Air Missile
AWACS	Airborne Warning and Control System
Bell	Extreme high angle of attack manoeuvre
C	Centigrade
CIS	Commonwealth of Independent States
cm^2	Centimetre Squared
Cobra	Extreme high angle of attack manoeuvre
DARE	Defence Avionics Research Establishment
DBS	Doppler Beam Sharpening
DRDO	Defence Research & Development Organisation
ECM	Electronic Counter Measures
EDCS	Electronic Distance Control System
ELINT	Electronic Intelligence
EW	Electronic Warfare
EWC	Electronic Warfare Controller
F	Fighter
FADEC	Full Authority Digital Engine Control
FBW	Fly By Wire
FCS	Flight Control System
FGR	Fighter Ground attack Reconnaissance
FWD	Forward
FX	Fighter Experimental
g	Gravity (1 g = 1 x Earth gravity)
G	Gravity (1 G = 1 x Earth gravity)
GLONASS	Globanaya Navigozionnaya Sputnikovaya Sistema (Global Navigation Satellite System)
GMTS	Ground Moving Target Selection
H	Height
HAL	Hindustan Aeronautics Limited
HMSS	Helmet Mounted Sight System
HMTDIS	Helmet Mounted Target Designation and Indication System
HMTDS	Helmet Mounted Target Designation System
HP	High Pressure
HRH	High Resolution mode
HUD	Heads Up Display

IAF	Indian Air Force
IAPA	Irkut Aircraft Production Association
IA-PVO	*Istrebitelnaya Aviatsiya Protivo-Vozdushnoy Obstrany*/Air Defence Force
IFF	Identification Friend or Foe
INS	Inertial Navigation System
IRST	Infra-Red Search and Track
ISIS	Islamic State (aka known as ISIL and Daesh)
JSC	Joint Stock Company
kgf	Kilogram Force
kg/s	Kilogram per second
km	Kilometre
km/h	Kilometre per Hour
kN	Kilo Newton
KnAAPO	Komsomolsk-on-Amur Aircraft Production Association
Kulbit	Extreme high angle of attack manoeuvre
KW	Kilo Watt
LERX	Leading Edge Root Extension
l/m	Litre per Minute
LP	Low Pressure
m	Metre
m^2	Metre Squared
Mach	Speed of Sound
MBDA	Matra British Aerospace Dynamics Alenia
MFDC	Multi-Function Display Screen
MFLCDS	Multi-Function Liquid Crystal Display Screen
MiG	Mikoyan
MKI	Modernised Commercial India
MKM	Modernised Commercial Malaysian
MODRF	Ministry of Defence of the Russian Federation
MRCA	Multi-Role Combat Aircraft
MRH	Medium Resolution mode
NATO	North Atlantic Treaty Organisation
NAVSTAR	Navigation Satellite Timing and Ranging System
OEPS	Optical Electronic Sighting System
OLS	Optical Location System
PESA	Passive Electronically Scanned Array
PFI	Advanced Frontline Fighter
POI	Probability Of Intercept
RAF	Royal Air Force
RB	Real Beam mode
RCS	Radar Cross Section
RMAF	Royal Malaysian Air Force
RWR	Radar Warning Receiver
s	Second (unit of time)

SAR	Synthetic Aperture Radar
SARH	Semi-Active Radar Homing
SEPECAT	*Societe, Europeene de, Production de1, Avion de Ecole de Combat et de' Appuie Tactique*
SOC	System of Objective Control
SS	Sea Search
Su	Sukhoi
Tail Slide	Extreme high angle of attack manoeuvre
TBO	Time between Overhaul
TV	Television
TWS	Track While Scan
UAV	Uninhabited Aerial Vehicles
US	United States
USAF	United States Air Force
UV	Ultra Violet
v	Velocity
WCS	Weapon Control System
x	Times (multiplication)
°	Degree
μ	Micron

ABOUT THE AUTHOR

Hugh, a historian and author, has published in excess of forty books; non-fiction and fiction, writing under his given name as well as utilising two different pseudonyms. He has also written for several international magazines, whilst his work has been used as reference for many other projects ranging from the aviation industry, international news corporations and film media to encyclopaedias, museum exhibits and the computer gaming industry. He currently resides in his native Scotland

Other titles by the Author include

Sukhoi T-50/PAK FA - Russia's 5th Generation 'Stealth' Fighter
Sukhoi Su-35S 'Flanker' E - Russia's 4++ Generation Super-Manoeuvrability Fighter
Sukhoi Su-34 'Fullback'
Sukhoi Su-30MKK/MK2/M2 – Russo Kitashiy Striker from Amur
Eurofighter Typhoon - Storm over Europe
Tornado F.2/F.3 Air Defence Variant
Boeing Super Hornet and Growler
Air to Air Missile Directory
North American F-108 Rapier – Mach 3 Interceptor
Convair YB-60 – Fort Worth Overcast
Boeing X-36 Tailless Agility Flight Research Aircraft
X-32 - The Boeing Joint Strike Fighter
X-35 - Progenitor to the F-35 Lightning II
X-45 Uninhabited Combat Air Vehicle
Into The Cauldron - The Lancaster MK.I Daylight Raid on Augsburg
Light Battle Cruisers and the Second Battle of Heligoland Bight
British Battlecruisers of World War 1 - Operational Log, July 1914-June 1915
Hurricane IIB Combat Log - 151 Wing RAF, North Russia 1941
RAF Meteor Jet Fighters in World War II, an Operational Log
Typhoon IA/B Combat Log - Operation Jubilee, August 1942
Defiant MK.I Combat Log - Fighter Command, May-September 1940
Blenheim MK.IF Combat Log - Fighter Command Day Fighter Sweeps/Night Interceptions, September 1939 - June 1940
Tomahawk I/II Combat Log - European Theatre - 1941-42
Fortress MK.I Combat Log - Bomber Command High Altitude Bombing Operations, July-September 1941
F-84 Thunderjet - Republic Thunder
USAF Jet Powered Fighters - XP-59-XF-85
XF-92 - Convairs Arrow

www.ingramcontent.com/pod-product-compliance
Lightning Source LLC
Chambersburg PA
CBHW041520220426
43667CB00003B/52